THE FUTURE OF BELIEF

THE FUTURE OF BELIEF

Theism in a World Come of Age

Leslie Dewart

HERDER AND HERDER

1966
HERDER AND HERDER NEW YORK
232 Madison Avenue, New York 10016
Fifth Impression 1967

Library of Congress Catalog Card Number: 66-26482

Manufactured in the United States

Contents

1.

Christian Theism and Contemporary Experience

THIS book attempts to sketch an approach to what may be among the most fundamental theoretical problems which challenge Christianity (and specifically the Catholic Church, with which I shall be predominantly concerned here) in the present age, namely, the problem of integrating Christian theistic belief with the everyday experience of contemporary man.

CHRISTIAN BELIEF AND CONTEMPORARY MAN

No small part of the difficulty may be that we have not, in our collective life as a Church, resolutely faced the problem. We perceive that there is a certain incongruity between Christianity and the contemporary world, but we frequently misconceptualize the precise nature of this lack of rapport. The first thing that requires emphasis, therefore, is that at its most basic level the problem is, as I have suggested, a *theoretical* one. It is hardly an essentially proselytic or pastoral matter, least of all a problem in public relations. In its ultimate import the problem *does* involve the self-communicating nature, eschatological aspirations and the missionary objectives of a faith which not unfittingly calls itself Universalism. But to suppose that the question of integrating Christian theism with contemporary experience is one of message-communication, how to convey the meaning of Christianity to a world whose ordinary human life renders it refractory to conversion—this would not only miss the real difficulty but would also include several assumptions contrary to fact.

It is not certain, for instance, that the mission of the Church can be properly described in terms of conveying an idea to those outside it. Christianity has a *mission,* not a *message.* The Gospel is not the textbook of the Christian faith; as *news* it is the report of an event that *happens.* To fulfill its mission, the creation of the Kingdom of God, and to achieve its role as the historical vehicle of God's self-communication to man, the Church must seek to extend itself to all mankind, and must therefore appeal, teach, preach and communicate itself. But what it communicates is its reality and existence, not an idea.

Nor is it clear, second, that if contemporary experience is an inhospitable environment for Christian belief, the reason has to do with the nature of that experience, either as contemporary or in relation to its specific content. To suppose that contemporary experience is, as such, a perversion of human nature is a hypothesis that does not have in its favour the benefit of *prima facie* validity. There is, after all, some logic to history. No doubt, man could pervert his own experience, but it is not readily apparent that science, for example, however proud and rebellious, is a radically mistaken mode of perception of the reality of man and world.

Third, it can be reasonably wondered whether some new rhetoric, however thoroughly reformed and recast, could be devised that would succeed in the enterprise of the world's conversion. The problem is not remotely one of, as it were, selling a product despite consumer resistance, a problem which the right technique of interpersonal manipulation might very well overcome.

Above all, finally, this conceptualization of the problem of the Church in the modern world would suffer from a serious confusion: *contemporary experience* should not be identified with the *non-Christian, non-believing experience* of those who are outside the Church. Implying as it would that contemporary experience as such is for the "others," this understanding of the problem would itself demonstrate that part of the difficulty may be a not uncommon (if also paradoxical and frequently unconscious) assumption that the *disintegration* of contemporary experience and Christian faith is, *up to a point,* the normal and natural state of affairs. What we really mean if we thus construe the project of integrating Christian belief and the everyday world, is that we hope that non-believing modern man will eventually cease experiencing himself and reality as he does, and that he will *replace* his contemporary experience with Christian belief. This would be the kind of "adjustment" of the Church to reality, the sort of "yielding" to the truth, that Karl Marx used to call a *mystification.*

Contemporary experience should rather be understood as the mode of consciousness which mankind, if not as a whole at least in respect of our own civilization constituting man's cultural vanguard, has reached as a result of its historical and evolutionary development. And the *integration* in question must be a true, organic process of co-ordination, interrelation and *unification.* To suppose that mankind could—or indeed should—voluntarily renounce its history, its normal development and its growth in self- and world-understanding would show an unrealistic and misguided lack of appreciation of the nature of man—if not also of that of the Christian faith. Likewise, the problem must refer to the contemporary *human* experience as such: the project of integrating faith and experience is at least as relevant to the contemporary experience of Christians (insofar as they have not deliberately subtracted themselves from the world of present reality) as to the experience of non-believers. In fact, if the solution to the problem should turn out to be useful towards the fulfillment of the missionary eschatological goals of the Catholic faith, the reason would be that the integration of Christian belief with the contemporary experience of *Christian* man automatically would integrate Christianity, at least in principle, with the experience of *any* contemporary man. Thus, even for the sake of their own success, narrowly proselytic endeavors must be subordinated to the wider, *theoretical* question of the integration of Christian belief with the contemporary state of human development.

Let us note, then, that the disparity between Christian theistic faith and everyday experience can be observed most immediately and instructively within the very heart of the Church. We all feel that not all is right with the present situation. To some of us this condition is painful; to others it is bitter-sweet. But regardless of what we may feel, we all observe that the fairly total and serene self-assurance which had long characterized the consciousness of the Catholic believer, has been shaken in recent years. We note that there is unrest, unease and a frequently undefinable dissatisfaction, among the faithful *and* the clergy. And though bishops do not often disclose to the Church as a whole what their everyday consciousness reveals, there are indirect signs that they too, though perhaps in a different way and for different reasons, experience uncertainties, limitations and inadequacies to a degree which they are not by tradition accustomed to suffer. This widespread restiveness accounts for the deluge of stormy metaphors about Peter's bark which has rained upon us since the end of Vatican II, and which confirms the dry reality of which I speak.

What has not been so generally remarked is three things. First, there is a noticeable pattern to these disturbances. Second, the disturbances are symptomatic manifestations, not aetiological factors, of the problem of relating belief and experience. Third, the pattern of symptomatic disturbances is associated with variations in the believers' participation in the typical experience of contemporary man.

The polarization of Catholic opinion into those who are exhilarated by the prospect of change and those who are fearful of it; into those for whom it is a primary concern that the faith of the people should not be "disturbed" and those who argue that the welfare of the Church, if not the conversion of the world, require radical innovations and possibly dramatic readjustments—these attitudes, as well as the multiple divisions of opinion on concrete issues such as, say, contraception, clerical celibacy, liturgical reform, the government of the Church, social involvement, peaceful co-existence, and so on, tend to cluster in such a manner that the terms *conservative* and *liberal* are, though highly imprecise in their literal meaning, perfectly intelligible and justified as designations of two quite different *attitudes,* two different *modes of thinking,* in contemporary Catholic life.

To be sure, no given *position* on any given subject marks anyone with one type of mentality or with another; it does not necessarily reveal one sort of attitude or the other. One is acquainted with a theologian who pioneered in ecumenism who, at last hearing, tended to uphold clerical celibacy. One knows of a possibly somewhat maligned cardinal who has fulminated, if not intrigued, against liberalization of the traditional position against contraception, who nonetheless favors nuclear disarmament and peaceful co-existence with Communism. It is not merely that there are exceptions, but that if one faces each issue with an independent enquiring mind, with intellectual autonomy and honesty, and on the matter's own merits, a proper and legitimate *random* divergence of conclusions is likely to emerge. But over and above this there is a pattern. It may well in part be that Catholics in the mass fail to approach each controversial question either on its own merits or in full consciousness of the fundamental principles which in point of fact are at play—it may be that they approach them with presuppositions which remain, if not below the level of consciousness, at least below the level of discussion. Whatever the reason, it is possible to estimate, not only that beyond liberal and conservative *positions* there are liberal and conservative *attitudes,* but also that these alternative modes of thinking correlate highly with a Catholic's degree of acquaintance with, participation in, and acceptance of, the contemporary modality of human experience.

For example, it is one thing to philosophize in the traditional Catholic manner. But it is another to imagine that since the specific difference of scientific enquiry is causal certitude, a perennial philosophy should satisfy the human mind more adequately than do the uncertainties and self-revisionism of modern science. The reasonableness of the first is certified by the long and honorable history of Scholasticism. But the second seems to ignore the reality of contemporary life. Whatever the human mind should or should not do, the contemporary experience includes *respect* for science—largely *because* of science's diffidence and its readiness to change its mind—whereas contemporary mans' enthusiasm for the self-assurance of much Catholic philosophical thinking is under much stricter control.

Similarly, it is one thing to believe that the ministry should be reserved to men. It is another to be influenced by the thought that "if women were capable of the priesthood, the Church would not have deprived them of this grace for so many centuries."[1] And it is one thing to conclude that artificial contraception is necessarily, always and intrinsically immoral. But it is quite another to argue that

> to maintain that it [the doctrine of Pius XI in *Casti Connubii*] could have been in the circumstances [namely, after invoking his right to speak in the name of the universal Church, divinely commissioned to preserve the integrity of moral life] erroneous doctrine would seem to impugn the very providence of God with respect to His Church and her ordinary teaching mission. In a matter so serious and of such general concern—literally a matter of eternal life or death for millions—could God conceivably have allowed His vicar, even on one occasion, to misinform the faithful so outrageously? And is it not even more incredible, even to the point of being theologically impossible, that God could have permitted an entire tradition of such teaching to develop and to continue uninterruptedly and unopposed for centuries? Practical faith simply cannot reconcile error of this magnitude with any meaningful guarantee of divine assistance "usque ad consummationem saeculi."[2]

To maintain the traditional practice against the ordination of women, or the traditional doctrine against the morality of contraception, is in itself not in the least unreasonable—indeed, these positions might well justly solicit the benefit of any reasonable doubt. But the mode of thinking that entered into the above

[1] Charles Boyer, as reported by *Slant,* I, 5 (Summer, 1965), p. 37.

[2] John J. Lynch, "The contraceptive issue: moral and pastoral reflections," *Theological Studies,* XXVII, 2 (June, 1966), pp. 258–259.

arguments, insofar as they proceeded *a priori* and dialectically from a clericalist concept of the Church which abstracted from the latter's historicity and from the fact that Christianity has a cultural form, does not immediately appear to have been deeply affected by contact with the world in which most people live.

If these observations are correct, it follows that the differences between "conservative" and "liberal" Catholic opinion today, in the specific sense of these terms assumed here, run considerably deeper than *liberals* have ordinarily admitted. The conservatives may have been closer to the mark when they have "alerted" the Church to a profound division within the Catholic faith. For these two ways of thinking manifest fundamental differences in one's most basic orientation towards the problem of the relation of the Catholic faith to the contemporary (and, indeed, to any given) stage of human development. We have to do here with divergent orientations towards the meaning of the Christian faith, towards the meaning of religion itself—and therefore towards the Catholic's very understanding of his self-disposition towards God. Ultimately, we may have to do with divergent conceptualizations of the God of Christian belief.

On the other hand, conservative opinion may not be correct in suspecting that this deep division within the Church points to someone's heresy. Both orientations seem to be perfectly possible within the strictest orthodoxy. (My reasons for this will be apparent below.) However, it also appears most probable that only one of these two ways of understanding the Christian faith is in point of fact theoretically the most adequate and practically the best suited to the present historical reality of the Christian faith—and that only one, therefore, can be profitably and beneficially retained.

It also follows, if the problem is truly of the character and magnitude I have suggested, that they would be mistaken who thought that the post-Vatican II critical period of the Catholic Church—hardly more than the first episode of which, probably, is behind us—can be accounted for in terms of what Pope John and the Council wrought (or loosed upon the Church, depending on one's viewpoint). Even Alexander Dru's judgment that "somewhere between the first Vatican Council and the second lies the watershed which divides the world of Pio Nono . . . from the present,"[3] appears to me an insufficiently generous estimate of what defines *contemporary* experience. What we are witnessing today might be more accurately envisaged as a resolution of the very problem of which the Reformation was an unfortunately abortive issue, namely, the integration of Christian belief with the *post-medieval* stage of human development. It may be no coincidence that the possibility of Protestant-Roman reunion, which we can now reasonably entertain for the first time since (if then) the days of Leibniz, coincides with the first real attempt of Catholic (as well as Protestant) Christianity to integrate Christian belief, and specifically Christian theism, with a human experience which is no longer remotely like that of the world in which that faith was born, or that of the world which that faith fashioned for itself when the world in which it was born collapsed and disappeared.

We have dealt with one possible misconception of the problem of modern experience and Christian faith, but there is another. We might mistake it for the problem of "the Church and the modern world," meaning the problem of reconciling the holy and the secular enterprises of man: God's religion *and* man's political organization, man's social life, man's economic existence,

[3] "From the *Action Française* to the second Vatican Council," *Downside Review,* LXXXI, 264 (July, 1963), p. 226.

man's technological world. The objection to this is not only that the opposition between theistic faith and everyday experience is not an opposition between the human and the divine, but also that the "outward" novelties and the "secular" changes that make up the contemporary world are but manifestations of a profound change in the mode and nature of human experience itself. The conceptualization of the problem as the integration of *faith* and *experience* is not a metaphorical way of speaking of the relations between *Church* and *world*. (After all, the Church is part of the contemporary world, which is the only real one.) On the contrary, it is the latter expression which is the metaphor. Thus, if the problem were understood as implicit in a question about the adaptations that the Catholic Church should make to the realities of a modern, industrial, technological culture, the answer would likely not go much beyond such matters as, say, the abolition of the eucharistic fast, the introduction of evening mass, acquiescence in the desuetude of "holy" days, the abandonment of the geographical parish, the ordination of women, the discontinuation of compulsory clerical celibacy, or perhaps the recognition that artificial contraception may contribute to the moral excellence of marriage—in a word, *aggiornamento,* with the concrete connotations of a vogue that this word has recently acquired. Obviously, such a question needs asking, and the replies, some of which have already been given, concern important matters. But the deeper question concerns an issue at once more fundamental and more comprehensive, namely, the meaningfulness of Christian belief for the experience and self-understanding of man in a modern, industrial, technological society. If we put it this way, the question looms considerably larger. For the experience and the self-concept of modern man do not merely fail to accord with institutional Christianity: they appear to conflict with Christianity's most basic doctrines and, in the first place, with belief in God.

It is the contemporary experience *as a whole* that is incongruous with Christian belief *as a whole.* Rudolf Bultmann has expressed this idea very graphically. It is very difficult for contemporary man, he has noted, to put together into a single mode of experience his *ordinary* Christian religious experience and the *trivial* experiences of every day, like reading a newspaper: or "have you read anywhere in [the newspapers] that political or social or economic events are performed by supernatural powers such as God, angels or demons?"[4]

But if the problem is not, on the one hand, the incorporation into belief of the trappings of modern civilization, neither is it, on the other, the integration of Christian belief with that specialized function of modern life which we call *science.* As the critics of ill-considered proposals to substitute science for belief often remind us, "the science of today is no longer the same as it was in the nineteenth century, and to be sure, all the results of science are relative, and no world-view of yesterday or today or tomorrow is definitive."[5] I am not certain that the conclusion would be different if scientific world-views were definitive, nor indeed (as I shall discuss in some detail below) that a "definitive" speculative foundation is what adequately establishes the truth and the relevance of Christian belief. At any rate—if not for better reasons, at least for the reasons given by Bultmann—it would make no sense to condition Christian belief upon the findings of science: "the main point, however, is not the concrete results of scientific research and the contents of a world-view," nor even—and here I part company with Bult-

[4] *Jesus Christ and Mythology,* (London, 1960), p. 37.
[5] *Ibid.*

mann—"the method of thinking from which world-views follow."[6] For science may well predominantly characterize the contemporary mode of experience, but it is not *science,* an extra- or super-human reality, that creates modern man. On the contrary, it is modern man that creates science. To be precise, modern man creates himself by means of science, that is, by means of his scientific mode of consciousness. For science is part of his self-creative endeavour. There is only a *figurative* sense, therefore, in which science does make man, namely, in the sense that it is *scientific culture* that defines *contemporary man*. Thus, what counts is neither the results nor the methods of science, but the human reality, the human experience and self-understanding, which produce the scientific method and scientific world-views, an experience and self-understanding which are then reciprocally molded by man's own scientific and other cultural creations.

It is in this sense that the typical contemporary experience can be said to be scientific, even if only a fraction of the population have more than an elementary acquaintance with science. Very few people in our culture would be able to give so much as an incoherent account of relativity theory, but all are affected by ballistic missiles and thermonuclear reactions; relatively few could tell the difference between the oral and the genital phases of psychosexual development, but relatively many could detect at least some rationalizations; and not many have heard of Cro-Magnon or Solutré, yet hardly anyone supposes that the Genesis account of creation is but a mythological one. It is not on science as such, but on the contemporary cultural stage of human self-consciousness, typically manifested in and conditioned by science and technology, that the traditional Christian faith grates.

[6] *Ibid.*

Now, the most common way for contemporary man to remain Christian and to believe in the Christian God is to retain, side by side, in relative though by no means complete isolation, two modes of experience, in the hope that somehow, in some way unknown to him, the two can be integrated. Or perhaps it should be put conversely: it is difficult for the contemporary Christian to experience the total and complete unity of religious experience and everyday existence. Most of those who remain faithful to the Christian tradition opt for this relative isolation as the best and most prudent compromise. But not a few opt for a more extreme course, namely, the rejection (in varying degrees, to be sure, and through a variety of mechanisms) of the validity, if not also the reality, of contemporary experience, in order to retain an integrally Christian religious experience.

The far greater majority of men in the West have, on the other hand, opted for the opposite extreme: the rejection (also, to be sure, in varying degrees) of the realism, if not also the moral validity, of "institutional" religion and, retaining an integrally contemporary experience, they have fashioned for themselves (if they have not drifted into religious indifference or discovered the religions of atheism) a vague religious sentiment more or less distantly affiliated to the traditional Christian belief to which, from the point of view of the history of culture, they continue to belong.

In brief, the problem is, at its most basic level, whether one can, while complying with the demand that human personality, character and experience be inwardly integrated, at one and the same time profess the Christian religion *and* perceive human nature and everyday reality as contemporary man typically does.

In his assumption that this is a contradiction in terms, Sigmund Freud spoke for modern man. His understanding of the matter deserves study, because his analysis established the focal point of the issue. It may be significant that in his most consequential work on religion, *The Future of an Illusion,* he did not substantially appeal to psychoanalytic theory. He appears rather to have reflected the fairly common attitudes of several generations of Western man.

RELIGIOUS BELIEF AND RELIGIOUS ILLUSION

Despite the civilizing and socializing effect on man with which religion may be credited, modern man—according to Freud—has gradually, almost by imperceptible steps, arrived at a realization which the psychologist would conceptualize more adequately in these terms: religion shows all the characteristics of that psychological process known as *illusion.* However, the term *illusion* is a technical one. It can be easily misunderstood. Freud "has often been accused of having in this book maintained that religious beliefs are untrue, illusory in the sense of nonexistent. And this in spite of his care to explain exactly in what sense he was using the term 'illusion', distinguishing it from error."[7] Freud stipulated that

> an illusion is not the same as an error, it is indeed not necessarily an error [though it may, of course, be also an error]. . . . It is to be distinguished from [delusion] . . . in which we [psychologists] emphasize as essential the conflict with reality . . . Thus we call a belief an illusion when wish-fulfilment is a prominent factor in its motivation, while disregarding its relations to reality, just as the illusion itself does.[8]

[7] Ernest Jones, *Sigmund Freud: Life and Work,* Vol. III, (London, 1957), p. 381.

[8] Sigmund Freud, *The Future of an Illusion,* (London, 1928), pp. 53–55. The syntax of the last sentence is awkward. The subject of *disregarding* is *we.*

If a man's psychic needs—principally the basic need to preserve a certain degree of psychological integration—are threatened by events or entities in reality, an illusionary wish-fulfillment may save him from psychological disintegration, at least until that time when his psychic development should permit him to cope with reality in a more adequate way. Like a fever, or like pain, illusions can be "healthy," that is, they can contribute to man's welfare. It is only in relation to a better state of affairs that they can be said to be symptoms of disease.

Now, since primitive times mankind has felt understandably helpless in the face of dangers to its existence and welfare, which are threatened by nature from without, and by man's inner conflicts and self-obscurity from within, and by the ambivalence of interpersonal relations, which unavoidably make other human beings the indispensable but obstructive, the rewarding yet frustrating, concomitant of human life:

> and so a rich store of ideas is formed, born of the need to make tolerable the helplessness of man, and built out of the material offered by memories of the helplessness of his own childhood and the childhood of the human race. It is easy to see that these ideas protect man in two directions: against the dangers of nature and fate, and against the evils of human society itself.[9]

The trouble with religion, and specifically with belief in God, is not that it must be necessarily false—Freud admitted to more than agnosticism on the point—nor even indeed that it is an infantile illusion. The trouble with religious theism is that, having once had an important, in fact, necessary role in human development, and having once usefully served man as a means of coping with utterly real perplexities, it has perpetuated itself beyond his needs. With increased self-consciousness and in-

[9] *Ibid.*, p. 32.

creased mastery of the world (both accomplishments remain, to be sure, highly imperfect), man can devise more adequate means than religion to grapple with the same problems. (Science is, of course, the principal, though by no means the only, such means.) Indeed, more than merely superfluous, the perpetuation of the religious illusion might become deleterious if it should retard the development of man. But, continues Freud, it can be hoped —in fact, it can be foreseen—that human progress will eventually assert itself. The only future that can be reasonably forecast for the illusion of belief is that the heightening of human consciousness will in due time dispel it.

Since Freud recognized that the problems to which the psychological mechanism of religious illusion responds are real, he implied that there might be deeper sources of religious experience than illusionary wish-fulfillment. But he also maintained that on the basis of common observation and of the analysis of religion as a cultural institution, in the experience of the majority of men in Western civilization the only discernible effective role of theistic belief was that of a psychological anodyne:

> The ordinary man understands by . . . religion, that system of doctrines and pledges that on the one hand explains the riddle of his world to him with an enviable completeness, and on the other assures him that a solicitous Providence is watching over him and will make up to him in a future existence for any shortcomings in this life. The ordinary man cannot imagine this Providence in any other form but that of a greatly exalted father, for only such a one could understand the needs of the sons of men, or be softened by their prayers and placated by the signs of their remorse. The whole thing is so patently infantile, so incongruous with reality, that to one whose attitude to humanity is friendly it is painful to think that the great majority of mortals will never be able to rise above this view of life.[10]

[10] Sigmund Freud, *Civilization and its Discontents,* (London, 1930), p. 23.

But in common with every other scientific humanist, Freud hoped that mankind might one day "rise above this view of life." He looked forward to the future when mature man should find it possible to

> do without the consolation of the religious illusion . . . [in order to] endure the troubles of life, the cruelty of reality. . . . Perhaps he, not suffering from neurosis, will need no intoxicant to deaden it. True, man will then find himself in a difficult situation. He will have to confess his utter helplessness and his insignificant part in the working of the universe; he will have to confess that he is no longer the centre of creation, no longer the object of the tender care of a benevolent providence. He will be in the same position as the child who has left the home where he was so warm and comfortable. But, after all, is it not the destiny of childishness to be overcome? Man cannot remain a child forever; he must venture at last into the hostile world. This may be called "education to reality"; need I tell you that it is the sole aim of my book to draw attention to the necessity for this advance?[11]

It is not my intention here to enter into polemics. On the contrary, I intend to show that Freud's observations are largely correct. But precisely because they are, it is necessary at least to mention certain points which appear to be not well founded. For in his argument Freud retained certain questionable presuppositions which do not invalidate his argument altogether, but which once exorcised require one to transpose his conclusions into a key that does not readily harmonize with scientific humanism.

In a certain respect the world-view represented by Freud did rise above that of "primitive" man (that is, of man up to the beginning of modern times). To that extent Freud was able to become conscious of the role which the "primitive" world-view had played in man's conceptualization of his situation in the

[11] *The Future of an Illusion,* pp. 85–86.

world and, thus, in the determination of the form of his religious belief. But in other basic respects Freud failed to surpass "primitive" man. To believe, for example, that the scientific *Weltanschauung* required the confession that man "is no longer the centre of creation," was to assume a relatively "primitive" and gross, indeed an inadequate and quasi-geometrical, criterion of the centrality of man's position in the universe. Similarly, Freud's view of human development was curiously static. His vision of the possibilities open to man was unduly restricted. His scientific humanism was, thus, insufficiently humanistic. Teilhard de Chardin has shown that, on the contrary, when coupled with the discovery of cosmic evolution, the experience of the spatio-temporal vastness of the universe reveals the new unsuspected dimension along which man's relation to reality should be measured, and the vastly grander scale on which should be rated man's position within the universe.[12]

Moreover, despite their scientific superiority to primitive man's, Freud's own feelings and attitudes towards reality were not sufficiently different in quality from those which underlay the religious illusion. The idea that man should *resign* himself to his "helplessness" and the view that man must learn to *brave* the "hostile" world betray an ambivalent dread which may go beyond the unalloyed emotions of man at an earlier stage of development, but which nevertheless assumes much the same *fear* of the world. With the greater self-confidence provided by his superior cultural equipment, Freud went beyond primitive man in proposing that fear should be overcome. But he did not appear to doubt that reality *is* truly frightening. He shared the primitive view that the apprehension of reality *should* normally

[12] "Life and the Planets," in *The Future of Man,* (London, 1964), 97–123.

elicit concern for one's safety. Like primitive man—according to Freud—contemporary man *is* bound by the nature of reality to experience "helplessness" when faced with the "cruelty" of the world. Therefore, Freud thought that man should *dare* to dispel the religious illusion which primtive man had earlier welcomed and put to good use. In short, he proposed that modern man should react differently to what he assumed to be the *same* situation in which both primitive and contemporary man find themselves by nature.

And yet, it may be that the possibilities open to man are much wider than Freud suspected. It may be that man's reaction *should* be different, but only because his situation is *not* the same. For it may be that to a mankind come of age the world should no longer appear hostile, but simply stimulating and challenging. There is no need to resign oneself to the loss of "consolation" if one does not stand in need of consolation in the first place. It may be that man need not be obsessed with the search for happiness if he should cease to see life as the source of inevitable "troubles," and if he should cease to experience the world as charged with hostility and anthropomorphic ill-will. The insecurity which Freud took to be natural to man may well be proper to only a passing stage of human evolution.

Man may not be *naturally* alienated. He may not be truly threatened by "the dangers of nature and fate." Or is it *a priori* unreasonable to wonder whether Freud's attitudes to reality were not themselves culturally and historically conditioned? There is indeed much evidence for the view that when Freud wrote that "the intention that man should be 'happy' is not included in the scheme of 'Creation',"[13] he did not merely mean that man is not assured of self-fulfillment and perfection by

[13] *Civilization and its Discontents,* p. 27.

nature but must instead creatively fulfill himself. He seems, rather, to have been harking back to a dominant theme of Greek philosophy—to which he owed so much in so many other respects—that man, against whom, as Hippocrates said, "all things conspire," is destined by fatal cosmic forces to suffer tragic distress. Freud's position, thus, was radical—perhaps radical enough for its time. But it may not be radical enough for today.

It is *not* out of the question to doubt that the large legacy of pessimism we have inherited from Greece must be an essential part of human nature. We may question whether it is imperative that we choose between "the tender care of a benevolent providence" and an inauspicious, fated "destiny" of man. If reality is experienced as reality, if the world is envisaged as man's home, and if the purposiveness of conscious existence is conceived as *being* and not as *being happy,* the future forecast by Freud for the religious illusion might well come true—but in the form of a further development of Christian theism, not in that of its disappearance. If we transcend the inadequacies of the position represented by Freud, the assumption of its truth should lead us more adequately to envisage the future of belief.

For Freud's work did bear on the focal point of the problem of integrating contemporary experience and Christian faith. Note that it would be pointless to object to Freud that not every religious experience can be explained away as wish-fulfillment, or that human contingency and the inexplicable factuality of actual reality cannot be simply dismissed in the name of psychoanalysis. The problems are real: whether we answer them with, say, the atheism of Heidegger, or with the economics of Lenin, Freud's thesis cannot be invoked in order to *do away* with the legitimacy of religious preoccupation. But I have already mentioned that Freud did not deny the reality of this dimension of religion, and carefully specified that he referred to the religious belief of "the ordinary man." What requires stress is that if this qualification is kept in mind, it is as difficult to disagree with Freud's portrayal of the role that in point of fact religion has come to fulfill in Western Christendom, as with Marx's assertion that, like opium, religion has in fact been placed by man at the service of a self-exploitative mode of social organization.[14]

If an extra-terrestial social scientist on a field trip to this planet were to report on Western Christendom's religious institutions he could hardly fail to note that, for all its complexities and subtleties, the natives' religion, at least as manifested by their ascertainable everyday experience and activities, revolved around the belief that the most consequential fact of life was the ultimacy, irrevocability and absoluteness of the alternative possibilities open to man in the world beyond the grave: eternal and utter bliss, or eternal and utter suffering. In fact, the believers very often put the matter in precisely such terms—though here it might be necessary to distinguish between the more and the

[14] There is more than a terminological similarity between Freud's and Marx's analyses of religion: "Religious distress is at the same time the expression of real distress and the protest against real distress. Religion is the sigh of the oppressed creature, the heart of the heartless world, just as it is the spirit of a spiritless situation. It is the opium of the people. . . . The abolition of religion as the illusory happiness of the people is required for their real happiness. The demand to give up the illusions about its condition is the demand to give up a condition which needs illusions. The criticism of religion is therefore in embryo the criticism of the vale of woe, the halo of which is religion," Karl Marx, *Introduction to the Critique of Hegel's Philosophy of Right* (1844), in Howard Selsam and Harry Martel (eds.), *A Reader in Marxist Philosophy: Selected Writings of Marx, Engels and Lenin,* (New York, 1963), p. 227.

less authoritative sources. The more popular (and therefore the more abundant) literature would manifest the idea in an extreme and gross form. It would pay relatively little attention to a most important distinction between "perfect" and "imperfect" religious motivation, that is, "perfect" and "imperfect love of God." But even the most authoritative sources would agree that, in the last analysis, even that "love of God" which resolved itself into precisely such expectations as Freud described, was sufficient unto "salvation," that is, it would serve for the attainment of "the soul's eternal happiness." The more sophisticated and considerate teachers (but also, incidentally, the less representative of what the majority actually believed) would exhibit a much subtler and highly qualified form of the same belief. But in the end, it would indeed come to much the same thing.

No less unexceptionable a Catholic thinker than Jacques Maritain has, though hardly in so many words, admitted that the Christian morality of beatitude (that is, happiness) can take the illusionary form described by Freud. Although "the theologians are perfectly clear on all this," (namely, on the fact that "Christian morality is a morality of beatitude, but first and foremost it is a morality of the divine Good supremely loved"), nevertheless, he has written, "popular preaching is *often* inclined to put the emphasis above all, *if not even, exclusively* on the joys of the reward and the pains of punishment.[15]

I have granted that there are differences between "the theologians" and "popular preaching." On the other hand, if Maritain meant to imply that the latter have essentially misunderstood the former, the suggestion should be rejected in fairness to both the truth and to "popular preaching." The

[15] *Moral Philosophy,* (London, 1964), p. 79. (Italics mine.)

"popular preaching" may be a simplified, possibly even an oversimplified, version of what "the theologians" and indeed the authoritative magisterium of the Church have taught. But it is not a corruption or contradiction of it. To think otherwise may be to suffer from self-mystification. For, with but the intervention of a period, Maritain went on to provide a philosophical justification for doing precisely what "popular preaching" has done:

> These [the joys of the reward and the pains of punishment] are truths which immediately stir our natural appetite for happiness and our natural fear of suffering. And even if one insists *only* on them, one can always *hope* that once the sinner is turned toward the subsistent Good from motives in which love of self hold first place, the living faith will thereafter make him spontaneously subordinate his own interest to God loved first.
>
> After all, one lends only to the rich. And the preachers of the Gospel feel themselves excused in advance if, in the arguments by which they *push* us toward salvation, they employ *without too much scruple* a kind of eudemonism, even hedonism, *at least ambiguous in character,* in the service of the love of God.[16]

Or is Maritain atypical of a long Christian tradition? Rather one suspects that the supreme preoccupation of "the preachers of the Gospel" with the "salvation" of the soul—in the specific sense of "going to heaven" and "avoiding hell"—is but a fairly faithful reflection of both Scholastic theology and of what the magisterium has taught since early (though possibly not primitive) Christian times. At least, there is little evidence of a tradition of either papal, or other authoritative teaching against what might well be called (in a slightly more precise term than Maritain's) *spiritual hedonism,* a tradition which the lower clergy have evaded or ignored. Nor is it clear that "the preachers" have, in their oversimplification of the doctrine, traduced the basic meaning of the best Scholastic thought.

[16] *Ibid.* (Italics mine.)

This is true, in the first place, of neo-Thomists, for whom "morals is the science of how man is to conduct himself so that the story of his life may have a happy ending."[17] But it is also true of their original source. According to St. Thomas, the fulfillment of man's perfection, that for the sake of which he exists, is happiness, since "happiness means the acquisition of the last end."[18] To be sure, man's fulfillment consists in a *spiritual* and indeed *supernatural* happiness, for the "cause or object [of man's happiness] is something uncreated [namely, God]."[19] But this refers to happiness considered in relation to its object as such. "If we consider happiness as to its very essence, then it is something created," that is, it is something "existing in him [that is, man], and this is nothing else than the attainment or enjoyment of the last end."[20] What, then, is the difference between this doctrine and classical hedonism? Are not the two indistinguishable? Not at all, according to St. Thomas, because that "happiness [which] is man's supreme perfection . . . must consist

[17] Etienne Gilson, *Moral Values and the Moral Life,* (London, 1931), p. 19.

[18] *Summa Theologiae,* [henceforth *ST*], I-II, 2, 1. St. Thomas's ethical doctrine rests on this principle. Though he would disagree with the conclusions that Greek philosophers derived from the same principle, since he imported into his philosophical thinking Christian beliefs and opinions, St. Thomas *based* his doctrine of morality on the Aristotelian idea that human purposiveness and striving are intelligible only in terms of a final cause—and this is the condition of the possibility of dissociating practice from theory, action from contemplation, the morality of life from the morality of death, and value from fact. Note also that Maritain's idea that Christian morality is *both* a morality of beatitude and "a morality of the Divine Good supremely loved," is impotent to show that the latter is really "first and foremost." He is ultimately reduced to *hoping* that out of a spiritual hedonism something better might emerge. The counter-suggestion offered to contemporary man by Marx and Freud is that the experiment has lasted long enough.

[19] *ST,* I-II, 3, 1.

[20] *Ibid.*

in man's last act."[21] Therefore, we can distinguish between two things, "happiness," and the "delight" taken in the attainment of happiness, a delight which is indeed "necessary for happiness," but which nonetheless is necessary for happiness only "as something attendant on it." The delight which we take in happiness, thus, is a mere "concomitant delight" which necessarily accompanies the "attainment of the Sovereign Good."[22]

One can understand the philosophical distinction between "happiness" and its "concomitant delight" and nevertheless sympathize with those who have to translate it into pastoral advice. This sympathy would have nothing to do with anyone's lack of sublety or with anyone's excess of it. It is simply that, if nothing else, the concomitance of happiness and delight logically implies that the attainment of delight (of the right sort, to be sure) can provide a practical criterion for the moral conduct of life. The adequacy of man's endeavor towards acquiring his due perfection and self-fulfillment can always in practice be judged by the adequacy of his search for ultimate and true bliss. Moreover, the distinction implies that there would be nothing basically wrong (though there would be something Christianly imperfect) with seeking ultimate delight for its own sake. This must be admitted not only in deference to common sense, but also theoretically. The delight taken in the acquisition of the object of happiness is a *necessary* concomitant of happiness. One *cannot* avoid taking delight in the attainment of self-fulfillment. It is *natural* for man to seek happiness with all his might. (And, moreover, who would dare say that it is orthodox Christian tradition that only "the perfect" can enter the Kingdom of Heaven—at least, by way of its purgatorial antechamber?) In

[21] *ST,* I-II, 3, 2.
[22] *ST,* I-II, 4, 1.

fact, once the distinction is accepted, even the spontaneous inclination of Christian humility and Christian realism might well foster the idea that "perfection" is not for *me,* the average man, who am aware of my weaknesses and cupidity, who try my very best to do what is right, who am disposed to do what I ought to do (whatever *that* might be) regardless of inconvenience, but who, not having had mystical experiences or the call that moves the saints, do not really *know* what it means to love God more than myself—unless perhaps it meant totally abdicating my freedom in favor of . . . whom? or what?

The doctrine of St. Thomas, in the last analysis, rests on the hellenic principle that man's perfection *is* happiness. Though man may "know not in what thing [namely, God] the general notion of happiness is found," it remains true that "to desire happiness is nothing else than to desire that one's will be satisfied."[23] If so, why should the preacher of the Gospel not con-

[23] *ST,* I-II, 5, 8. Since in the following chapters I will not be concerned with ethical questions, not wanting to omit constructive suggestions altogether I would briefly indicate a possible alternative fundamental principle of ethics. This principle would convey the idea that the moral self-fulfillment of man is intrinsically connected with his ontological self-realization rather than with his affective reaction to reality as an object set off from him. The ontological perfection of man, his free and self-creative coming-into-being, overflows into moral perfection because man does his existing in the presence of God. What man makes himself to be, therefore, places him in a certain existential situation in relation to God. Man's purposiveness and striving, thus, reside in his seeking creatively, not to be *happy,* but to *be*. The Christian doctrine of grace can be totally integrated with this idea if we keep in mind that the free self-creation of man takes place in the presence of God not only insofar as it constitutes man's *final* achievement, but also insofar as it constitutes his constant, *present* being. (In Scholasticism, if man were immortal and remained on earth forever, morality would be very difficult to understand). Man's *present* self-creation takes place in the *presence* of God *as* communicating himself to man. Thus, in opposition to Scholasticism this concept of morality stresses the creativity and the presentness of morality,

tinue to recommend the sweets of "perfection," but prudently and realistically settle for concern with the staples of the moral life?

Of course, this is not the whole of St. Thomas's doctrine; there is much that thoroughly qualifies it. But I am not aware of any other doctrine of St. Thomas which retracts this position, nor indeed, of any other doctrine which he offers under the guise of a *theoretically* more basic nature. The last point is to be emphasized, because there is no reason to believe that in his own personal life St. Thomas, any more than those who have agreed with him, actually abided by this hedonism. One can only suppose that he *lived* an integrally Christian conception of morality, namely, the sort "which seeketh not her own."[24] It is because he *was* a saint that one can be morally certain that St. Thomas did not practice what he preached. This is but another way of saying that the integration of faith and reason in Scholasticism is less than perfect. Whenever St. Thomas explicitly or implicitly supposed that man's perfection and self-fulfillment consisted in something other than the acquisition of happiness in the possession of an objective end, he proposed, in effect, a view which was truly Christian, but which could not be reconciled with the hellenic approach to ethics which he had taken in his more fundamental speculative work.

It is this lack of integration that enabled Maritain to exculpate "the theologians" at the expense of "the preachers." Perhaps it would be closer to the truth to admit that the eudemonism of

---

but in opposition to certain contemporary philosophies it stresses that the present self-creation of man takes place in the presence of God, so that we are judged according to what we make of ourselves, not in the sense that our final achievement is measured by an ideal standard, but in the sense that what we do make of ourselves does make a real difference to our moral relations with God.

[24] 1 Cor. 13, 5.

"the preachers of the Gospel" is but a consequence—though perhaps also an exaggeration—of the cardinal, albeit somewhat inconsistent, spiritual hedonism of Scholasticism. It is for *this* reason that "the preachers of the Gospel" might well feel themselves excused upon further reflection. For the minister's task is, after all, a practical one. In the end it is the pastor who has to dissolve the inconsistencies and liquidate the mystifications of theologians and philosophers. The Catholic clergy have generally attempted but to convey to the faithful, as best they could, the mind of the Church. The difficulty is that ever since Christian morality began to be conceptualized (to use St. Thomas's own language again) in terms of the performance of "certain acts" which constituted the "means" whereby "happiness is to be gained,"[25]—in other words, ever since it began to be cast in the hellenic concepts of *means* to the attainment of a *final end*—it has been difficult to preach Christianity without fostering the illusion described by Freud.

But this is not the proper occasion to settle the question of the origins of that spiritual hedonism whose fountainhead, in any event, antedates St. Thomas by a thousand years, and which Scholasticism merely canalized. What must be stressed above all is that this spiritual hedonism exists, not indeed as an isolated phenomenon, not as heresy, not as deviation from the norm, but as characteristic of the current form of our faith. One is happy to admit that we are not, in our best moments, reconciled to it, and that though we have long and willingly lent ourselves to it we have not completely succumbed to it. Our reluctance to avow it openly is the best token of the fact. But spiritual hedonism is the most frequent component of the religious experience of "the ordinary man," not because he, any more than

[25] *ST*, I-II, 6, *prooemium*.

the clergy, has betrayed theology or the magisterium—nor, for that matter, because theology or the magisterium has betrayed the Church—but simply because under certain historical and cultural conditions this was the logical way (*perhaps* even, relatively speaking, the best way) in which the truth of Christianity could be cast. For Maritain was not mistaken to think (if this is what he really had in mind) that if the Church has believed in and taught a doctrine which at a later time might be inadequate, for all that the Church has carried the torch of truth and brought to man the light of God. But Maritain may not have been correct in attributing the inadequacy to one part of the Church, when in reality it pertained to the Church as a whole.

But even the inadequacies of the Church as a whole must be properly understood. Not even Freud sought to *blame* anyone for the religious illusion. But we might go beyond Freud and insist that it was not only "healthy," but also *proper* and *good,* under concrete historical and cultural conditions for Christian theism to have taken the "illusory" forms it has. No one need, or indeed should, regret having lived a younger life, no one need be ashamed if when he was a child he spoke as a child. But, if not with Freud, then with another Jew whom Freud admired,[26] we might agree that once we admit to ourselves that we are no longer children, the time has come to "put away the things of a child."[27] Perhaps one of the first things to put away is the illusion that the illusion does not exist.

If any doubt should remain on the point, perhaps we might, finally, enquire from those who today are concerned "lest the faith of the people should be disturbed," whether the disturbance

[26] Cf. Ernest Jones, *op. cit.,* p. 377.
[27] 1 Cor. 13, 11.

they fear is that the faithful should bestir themselves and undergo, in this life, the real sufferings of freedom accepted and responsibility faced, the true discomfort of adolescent pain, the arduousness of creative endeavor, the turmoil which accompanies all human development, but particularly the re-organization of one's self-concept and the conscious re-disposition of one's life—or whether what they really fear is that the faithful might, through loss of faith in *whatever* concept of Christianity they might now possess, endanger their eternal happiness in the world to come. If so, they may find, though surely not a moral, some amusement in an old Catholic story recently retold by Eugene Fontinell.[28] It concerns a legendary saint "who encountered an angel walking down the road with a torch in one hand and a pail of water in the other. When asked what they were for he replied, 'The torch is to burn down the castles of heaven and the water to put out the flames of hell and then we shall see who really loves God'." What is most enlightening in this bit of Catholic folklore is not that we do not really believe it—but that although the literary form marks the tale as a "primitive" one, its sentiment is very much in the spirit of contemporary man.

It should not be necessary to state that the observations recorded here, as well as the conclusion that Christian belief in its traditional form is at its most basic level not attuned to the contemporary experience of man (and, conversely, that the contemporary stage of human self-consciousness is not conducive to Christian belief in its traditional form) have been often made, even by Catholic thinkers, before now—though, as I have suggested, the problem is sometimes misconceptualized in sev-

[28] "Reflections on faith and metaphysics," *Cross Currents,* XVI, 1 (Winter, 1966), p. 40.

eral different ways. In fact, it would not be an exaggeration to judge that the most significant developments in Christian speculation in the twentieth century—certainly the most influential concepts and the most interesting movements—have had more or less directly to do with this problem. What, then, beyond the conceptualization of the problem offered above, does this book propose to contribute to the study of the question?

CONTEMPORARY THEOLOGY AND THE CONCEPT OF GOD

This book advances, first, the suggestion that the integration of Christian belief and contemporary experience must logically begin—that is, it cannot in the end abstract from—the integration of the *concept of God* with contemporary experience. The point would seem elementary, given the central and basic position of theism within the Christian religion. Surely, if any part of the Christian faith must be in perfect harmony with everyday life it must be this. Conversely, would it matter very much if Christian belief were an integral part of contemporary human experience in every respect except in what concerned belief *in God?* And yet, the greater part of the considerable effort of recent Christian speculation has been concentrated on collateral issues. The direct treatment of the problem of everyday experience and Christian belief *in God* has been relatively neglected, even if it is amply recognized that "we unquestionably do need a re-statement of what God is all about."[29] No doubt, this neglect is largely but the obverse of the relatively great advances made in logically posterior, yet possibly more immediately pressing, areas of research. Obviously, we can proceed only step by

[29] Herbert McCabe, Review in *New Blackfriars,* XLVI, 543 (September, 1965), p. 698.

step. My suggestion, thus, merely means: the time has come for Christian thought to apply itself, within its more general plan to integrate experience and faith, to the problem of the concept of God.

But beyond the fact that what is logically prior need not be investigated first, it may be that the very central and fundamental nature of theism within the Catholic faith has tended to discourage the application of the Christian intellect to any possible readjustment of its theistic doctrines, and this on the conscious or unconscious assumption that here, if nowhere else, we find an absolutely immutable Christian concept. The problem of integrating theism and modern life requires, therefore, a theoretical justification (in the light of a commitment to the *truth* of Christianity) of the *attempt* to integrate it with contemporary experience—in other words, a theory of dogmatic development.

In any event, whatever may be the other reasons why the re-examination of the concept of God tends to be delayed, one of them is well illustrated by the otherwise baffling disparity between the "liberalism" of a theologian such as Paul Tillich in every other respect, and his traditionalism—indeed, to use his own adjective, his "Scholastic" conservatism—in his final doctrine concerning the nature of God.

Tillich himself admitted in the end that for all his avoidance of the word God, for which he had frequently substituted "the ground of being," what he really meant was nothing else than that which

> in the tradition of the classical theology of all centuries we call God—or, if you prefer, "being itself" or "ground of being." And this "being" does not merely exist and is not merely essential but transcends that differentiation, which otherwise belongs to everything

finite . . . [But] it is not necessary [to talk about a ground of being]. I would prefer to say "being itself." But I know that this term is even more disliked [than "God"]. And so I speak of the ground of being. I actually mean, with the classical theologians, being itself. . . . "Ground" is of course a metaphor. And it is a metaphor which actually points to the idea of creation, to the symbol of creation. . . . However, if I were able to go back to the scholastic term *esse ipsum,* I would prefer that.[30]

Tillich's contribution to the cause of bringing the Christian faith to its proper level of contemporary self-awareness cannot be belittled, and I would here but echo the appreciation of his work made by George Tavard and other Catholic scholars.[31] However, it appears that Tillich did not reach the root of the problem of experience and faith, and that in this precise, if limited, sense his theology is insufficiently radical. On the other hand, Tillich was no more perfectly consistent than any other human being. There are innumerable passages in the first volume of his *Systematic Theology* and in *The Courage to Be* where "the ground of being" and the "ultimate reality" are distinctly not the equivalent of *esse ipsum*. In fact, throughout most of Tillich's theology the concept of God is not that "of all centuries," but that of a reality which transcends being and, specifically, one which transcends both essence and existence. But when he was pressed to face the question of the nature of God, Tillich found it ultimately necessary to revert to the "classical" position. The transcendence of God means that there is in him no distinction between essence and existence. But however ultimate and transcendent, God's reality, if he is a reality, must be conceived as *being*. And insofar as God's prin-

[30] *Ultimate Concern* (New York, 1965), pp. 45–46.

[31] George Tavard, *Paul Tillich and the Christian Message,* (New York, 1962); Thomas A. O'Meara and Celestin D. Weisser (eds.), *Paul Tillich in Catholic Thought,* (Dubuque, 1964).

cipal and original relation to man is that of creator to creature, God must be conceived as the being who is the *cause* of being.

This may mean that Tillich's doctrine of God is really ambivalent. Its ambivalence is definable by the twofold aptness of the concept "the ground of being" to mean, on the one hand, the Scholastic subsisting Being Itself, in whom essence and existence are real and identical, and, on the other, a doctrine that, at least for the Catholic thinker, can have only "a depressing effect, for it seems to equate God with the basic energy at work in the universe, but interpreted in terms of human concern."[32]

This ambivalence may, in turn, account for Tillich's understanding of the Trinity in a manner which could not be easily fitted within the Catholic tradition, insofar as it would reduce the distinction of Persons to a more or less figurative, symbolic distinction among the various human relations to the one God—his Christology would be, if anything, somewhat less reconcilable with the Catholic understanding of what is essential to belief in the Incarnation of the Word. At least, one could conclude this from the observation that there seems to be some disparity between Tillich's use of a certain philosophical orientation in relation to some theological problems, and his use of a different (or no) philosophical orientation in relation to others. Much of his theology was based on a concept of God which lacked the traditional philosophical notes it has had in the "theology of all centuries": this is what made possible his understanding of many Christian doctrines in close integration with contemporary experience. But when he was pressed to face directly the question of the nature of God *and* the interpretation of the Christian doctrines of the Trinity and the Incar-

[32] Gustave Weigel, "The theological significance of Paul Tillich," in *Paul Tillich in Catholic Thought,* p. 17.

nation, the borrowed categories of strict phenomenology and of subjective existentialism no longer served him well in *both* respects simultaneously. His integration of faith and experience sundered the concept of God from the Christian dogmas of the Trinity and the Incarnation. His interpretation of the latter *was* integrated with contemporary experience—but, it would seem, at the price of transcending the traditional Christian faith concerning God. His concept of God, on the other hand, bore the whole burden of carrying the Christian faith—at the price, evidently, of reverting to Scholasticism[33] and, thus, jeopardizing at a fundamental level the project of integrating contemporary experience and Christian belief. In sum, for all his *concessions* to contemporary experience, Tillich was ultimately swayed by a philosophical prejudice which in the end separated him from the experience of contemporary man: the idea that reality as such is properly, necessarily and exclusively conceivable as *being,* or otherwise not at all.

Hence, this book advances, second, the suggestion that the integration of Christian belief and contemporary experience, especially in what concerns the concept of God, could not be successfully attempted by a Christian theology which, however radical and novel in every other respect, assumed any fundamental principle or essential part of that very mode of philosophical enquiry (and particularly the classical epistemologies and metaphysics) on which was erected the concept of God which can no longer be integrated with contemporary experience.

But perhaps this should be put positively. The integration of

[33] It may be significant that Tillich finally reverted to the *Scholastic* notion of God. Some observations to be made below should suggest that this concept of God naturally lends itself to being severed from the Christian doctrines of the Trinity and the Incarnation.

faith and experience might be successfully undertaken, particularly with regard to the central dogmatic theism of the Catholic faith, in the light of philosophical principles which in their totality corresponded to the contemporary level of human self-consciousness. In other words, the adoption of an existential anthropology side by side with a traditional (or no) theory of knowledge and a traditional (or no) ontology, is not a harbinger of success. For if the project of integrating faith and contemporary experience is going to be ultimately successful, it must be sufficiently radical. To be sufficiently radical it must get to the root concept of God. And to be sufficiently radical respecting the conceptualization of God, it must radically depart from the philosophic world-viewing which has given the traditional Christian faith in God a cultural form which no longer serves well that Christian faith.

In one respect, therefore, the thought of Dietrich Bonhoeffer should be considered—despite its incomplete and sketchy nature which hardly compares favorably with the monumental work of Tillich—an improvement over Tillich's basic doctrine. For Bonhoeffer recognized clearly two things: (a) that if, rejecting fideism as well as the dichotomization of faith and experience, we project the integration of Christian faith and contemporary experience, then contemporary experience must be accepted *as given* and *as an integral whole;*[34] and (b) that, therefore, no part of the Christian faith, not even the concept of God, should escape re-examination and re-conceptualization at the most fundamental level.[35] Bonhoeffer did not live to suggest more

[34] This is surely the important principle behind Bonhoeffer's idea of "Christianity without religion."

[35] This is surely the truth that has been inflated by rhetoric in certain circles of the post-Bonhoeffer movement—though a truth which its critics have not always fully recognized. Herbert McCabe's assessment

concretely and positively what form Christian theism might take once it accepted the fact that "a world thus come of age . . . [could] live without the tutelage of God'."[36] This means we can only speculate as to what he might have ultimately contributed if his thought had had the opportunity to develop and mature. (It has also meant that Bonhoeffer's thought has been at the mercy of his followers.) The suggestion of this book is that it is precisely at this level that a Christian philosophy could usefully intervene in Christian theological speculation.

In their recognition of the need for Christian theism to accept as given the contemporary experience and to feel itself free to accept novel philosophical foundations, Bonhoeffer and Teilhard de Chardin can be appropriately paired. Teilhard's thought was not an apologetic endeavor to "harmonize" science and the traditional conceptualizations of the Christian faith. It was a creative attempt to follow through to its ultimate consequences a scientific and fully contemporary (scientific) experience in the light of a Christian faith which, on the one hand, functioned to make that scientific experience religiously meaningful, but which, on the other, required re-interpretation and re-conceptualization in the categories of contemporary experience for the very sake of illuminating that everyday scientific experience.

But, once again, if there are certain aspects of Teilhard's vision which might be seriously questioned in relation to their faithfulness to the truth of Catholic belief—and I believe there are some—we could trace the difficulty to a certain philosophical

---

(*art. cit.*) of recent theological debates in this vein introduced much good sense into the discussion, as did Justus George Lawler's "Theology and the uses of history," *Continuum,* IV, 1 (Spring, 1966), 92–101 (though my disagreement with the latter at certain points should be clear from the next chapter).

[36] *Letters and Papers from Prison,* (London, 1953), p. 146.

weakness which, however understandable and excusable, does mar his seminal thought. For instance, there are several passages in Teilhard that only with great difficulty, if at all, could escape the objection that in his doctrine the evolutionary processes lead *necessarily* and *inevitably* to a final (Omega) point of history.[37] For Teilhard occasionally equated intelligibility and necessity—and a Christian can do so only as long as he does not believe in evolution.[38] Elsewhere, in postulating that "consciousness . . . is a universal property common to all corpuscles constituting the Universe, but varying in proportion to the complexity of any particular molecule,"[39] Teilhard was needlessly betrayed by an uncharacteristic reversion to a hellenic idea: that development must be reducible to becoming, that is, to the act of that which is in potency insofar as it is in potency—and that, therefore, in things which develop the actual is intelligible only in

[37] *The Future of Man,* (London and New York, 1964), pp. 57, 147, 152.

[38] That is, the Christian can equate intelligibility and necessity (and, thus, adopt a hellenic philosophical viewpoint) only as long as he also understands becoming in a consequent manner, that is, as long as he conceives becoming as the act of (actually potential) being. But if he understood becoming as the act of (non-being) coming-into-being, that is, as the act of something "coming" (or, rather, being) *from nothing,* (which he must do if evolution and development are to be understood, in turn, as the emergence of something which is not ultimately reducible to its antecedents), the identification of intelligibility and necessity would necessarily lead to conclusions which, as I believe, could not be subsumed under Christian belief (for example, the evolutionary nature of God and his pantheistic identification with nature). The reluctance of Catholic speculation to accept the concept of evolution except in carefully delimited (and occasionally mystifying) respects, may be accounted for by (a) its conscious or unconscious assumption of the incompatibility I have just described, and (b) its simultaneous conscious or unconscious disposition to *retain* as an absolutely basic philosophical principle the hellenic identification of intelligibility and necessity (and indeed, the identification of these two with being as such).

[39] *The Future of Man,* p. 130.

relation to the possible. If so, there is at bottom *nihil novum sub sole*. That which results from evolution must be found in potency in that from which it evolves.[40]

Moreover, if we put together these two notions, the result would bring Teilhard uncomfortably close to an understanding of evolution as a Hegelian self-creation of the Absolute Spirit.[41]

[40] More precisely, in this philosophical tradition potency is essentially relative to act and is for the sake of act, *potentia dicitur ad actum*. Potency is, therefore, intelligible in relation to act. But this is true *simpliciter loquendo*, not necessarily *secundum quid*. For instance, potentiality is *prior to act* in the order of material causality, even if the potentiality of matter (insofar as it is entitatively an *actual reality*) presupposes the actuality of the First Cause who created it. Likewise, the intelligibility of all that is intelligible depends ultimately on its essential relation to the "divine ideas," which are identical with a God who is Pure Act. But within their own order, material things, things which develop, are, *as such*, intelligible only in relation to the *prior* potentiality from which their actuality is educed. To be sure, this prior potentiality is (a) the potency of something *in act*, since potency to being cannot exist except in that which actually is; and (b) the *actually real* potency of some being in act, so that the axiom still holds. But, indeed, *becoming* is the act of that which is in potency precisely *as such, prout in potentia*. The development of anything which develops is intelligible only insofar as it is *pre-determined* by the potency of that from which it develops.
The most fundamental assumption involved here is, of course, that *ex nihilo nihil fit*. This is a view that Greek philosophers were in *no* way able to transcend, and which Christian philosophers so far have been able to transcend only in *one* way, namely, in respect of God's creative causality (though we need not suppose, at the other extreme, that it need be transcended in *every* way).

[41] Rosemary Reuther's criticism of Teilhard's eschatology on these very grounds (Letter, *Commonweal*, LXXXIV, 12 [June 10, 1966] p. 345), appears to me completely valid. But she also judges that every evolutionary eschatology must be Hegelian. She appears to believe, moreover, (a) that any Christian eschatology must be dualistic (my term), at least in the sense that there is a necessary "real clash and antagonism between . . . the primal creation . . . which God . . . saw that it was 'very good' . . . and 'this world' . . . which falls below the good creation of God"; and (b) that my general agreement with Teilhard's evolutionary eschatology commits me to "nothing but a Hegelianism which makes

Though this aspect of Teilhard's thought is probably not central or decisive or definitive part of the spirit of his doctrine, there can be little doubt that Teilhardism is philosophically weak. But this does not mean it should be rejected. It means that the present moment of the history of the Church offers to the Catholic intellect the task of providing a rigorous philosophical foundation for such Christian visions as that which was inspired in Teilhard de Chardin by scientific experience.

Now, the estimate made here, that there are unresolved difficulties in recent Christian attempts to integrate theistic belief with contemporary experience, has depended very largely on the observation that despite its otherwise valuable contributions, this order of Christian scholarship has been hampered either by the assumption of philosophical foundations which almost by definition (and, in any event, by performance) are incongruous with contemporary experience—or else by the absence, total or partial, of suitable philosophical foundations developed to contemporary specifications and acceptable to Christian belief. It might be objected, however, that this assessment surely overlooks the thought of Rudolf Bultmann and others associated with his name.

We doubtlessly find in Bultmann a relatively rare transcendence of conscious or unconscious philosophical assumptions which are not in accordance with contemporary existence or which abstract from the contemporary level of human self-awareness. However, Bultmann has not actually developed, even in outline form, a dogmatic theology which would attempt to integrate the Christian dogmatic faith—or specifically Christian

---

everything that *is* good, and does away with the iconoclastic power of the Christian hope." The last chapter of this book may tend to substantiate my opinion to the contrary in all these respects.

theism—with the contemporary experience. Whether simply because his specialized scholarship is all scriptural, or because he actually supposes that dogmatic theology could be reduced to an abstract form of hermeneutics, the fact remains that Bultmann has attempted to integrate no more than the Christian's *reading of Scripture* with his contemporary everyday experience. Whatever the real fruitfulness of Bultmann's work—like many other exciting advances in exegesis and other areas of scriptural research made in recent times—his project of *demythologization* creates several dogmatic problems for each scriptural one it solves. And, to be candid, very specially for those Christians for whom "free examination" is not the unique source of dogmatic belief, the thought of Bultmann and the concept of demythologizing must be considered, though singularly stimulating, insufficient—indeed much too narrow—to respond adequately to the needs created by the problem of experience and faith as outlined above.

Perhaps the same point should be made rather more generally, in terms of certain significant differences (surely not surprising) between the typical difficulties with Catholic and Protestant attempts, respectively, to integrate theology and exegesis with contemporary experience. The differences are, as it so happens, related to their typically divergent traditional attitudes towards philosophy.

Speaking very generally, it can be said that Protestant thought is not well disposed towards philosophy. The traditional Protestant tendency to rely on Scripture alone predisposes it towards this attitude, which is confirmed by its original aversion to Scholastic rationalism. Catholic thought, on the other hand, has always recognized amply the indispensable role of philosophy in theological speculation. But in this context philosophy has to date continued to mean predominantly an obsolete mode of thought.

Hence, Protestant scholarship has excelled in scriptural studies, but systematic theology has never been its *forte*. And what there has been of the latter has tended to base itself as little as possible on philosophy and to favour an approach through scriptural meditation. *Radical* Protestant theology has been characterized by a variation of the same idea of dogmatic theology: it has tended to become the understanding of Scripture in the light of contemporary knowledge, and in particular science, history or modern philosophy. Yet, whereas exegesis in the light of, say, contemporary historical research techniques and with the aid of archaeology, philology, etc., has been an unqualified boon, exegesis in the light of contemporary philosophy has produced ambiguous results. For example, understanding the New Testament as a document which under rigorous scientific examination can reveal its original cultural and historical meaning, has led us to a deeper appreciation of the *total* humanity of Jesus and to an eye-opening assessment of the cultural and historical origins of the Christian faith. The contemporary philosophical understanding of human nature could in turn help much, for instance, towards more adequately than ever grasping the nature of the commitment required of the Christian in relation to the person of Jesus historically understood. But if, at the same time, in the absence of ready-made concepts of God which can be plundered from the classical sources of phenomenology and existentialism, God remains understood in the traditional way "of all centuries," say, as the *Supreme Being,* the Christian doctrine of the Incarnation is apt to become, if not totally impossible, so obscure as to be next to meaningless. In this approach, the integration of experience and faith has sometimes meant only the rhetorical and figurative re-interpretation of the traditional doctrine.

The opposite extreme tendency in Catholic thought has brought us an ever-widening gap between scriptural studies and dogmatic theology—an alarming gap that is much too well known and recognized to require further comment.[42] One can feel more sanguine about it than about the Protestant developments to which I have alluded above only because the situation is rapidly nearing impossibility. The dissociation of recent exegesis and systematic theology, insofar as the latter has remained predominantly Scholastic, has become almost unbearable. The end of this situation, somehow, must be supposed to lie just below the horizon.

In the light, thus, of this analysis of some of the difficulties of both the typically Protestant and the typically Catholic approaches to the problem, this book advances, finally, the suggestion that the basic methodological concept which Christian philosophy might use in order to integrate Christian theism and contemporary experience must be sufficiently comprehensive to deal, beyond the strictly scriptural aspect of the problem, with its dogmatic and historical dimensions.

More concretely, it will be suggested that the integration of theism with today's everyday experience requires not merely the *demythologization of Scripture* but the more comprehensive *dehellenization of dogma,* and specifically that of the Christian doctrine of God. Of course, this task is of such magnitude that I wish to reiterate what I mentioned in the opening paragraph of this introductory chapter: in this book I am merely sketching

[42] Cf. Karl Rahner, "Exegese und Dogmatik," *Stimmen der Zeit,* LXXXVI (1960–61), 241–262.

the proposal in broad outline, in order to try it on the touchstone of public examination.

Dehellenization is the negative way of expressing this idea. It is the logical term to use for it if, astride the present, before we proceed forward we take stock of where we have come from and where we have been. But we look to our hellenic past in order to transcend the ambivalent present. This transcending of the present is *dehellenization* insofar as the present is out-of-the-past. For this reason it is more difficult to find the logical name for that which dehellenization positively seeks to bring about. It is difficult to know what the future might look like as a result of the transcendence of the present, and as long as dehellenization is a project of the present, the future has not yet come about. On the day when we can call *dehellenization* by its correct present designation, as having transcended the past, the problem will be how to transcend *it*—whatever *it* might be called. Nonetheless, on the basis, not of what it might positively look like in the future, but of what its positive function at present already suggests, dehellenization may well be described, without a negative reference to the past, as the conscious historical self-fashioning of the cultural form which Christianity requires *now* for the sake of its *future*. In other words, dehellenization means, in positive terms, the conscious creation of the future of belief.

These three objectives taken together add up to the following thesis. Unlike Freud, this book deems that theistic belief has not only a past but also a future role in the evolution of man as he becomes increasingly self-conscious and civilized. But the complement of the thesis is that, quite in keeping with Freud's (and Marx's) analyses, the future of Christian theism is likely to depend on whether it chooses to contribute to the heightening of man's self-understanding and to the perfection of his "education to reality." This would in turn imply that Christian theism should first become conscious that its traditional form has necessarily and logically been childish and infantile to the very degree that it corresponded to an earlier, relatively childish, infantile stage of human evolution. Theism in a world come of age must itself be a theism come of age. There is, of course, nothing unusual, mistaken or shameful in the implication that theistic belief should have once been infantile. There might well be, however, something unreasoning, to say the least, in a theistic belief that willfully and consciously chose to remain forever out of phase with the maturity of human experience at any given stage.

To this end, in the next chapter I attempt to characterize that which in Christian theism puts it in conflict with its diametrically opposite contemporary experience, namely, atheism. I find this characteristic to be theism's supposedly necessary *absolute* form. Against the implication that the Christian doctrine of God might transcend its present absolute form, I ask in Chapter III the more general and procedural question whether Christianity is indissolubly wedded to its original (or to any given) conceptual form of its dogmas, to which I reply in the negative. In Chapter IV I then consider certain inadequacies that Christian theism has acquired in the course of time and by reason of man's cultural change. In the last chapter I suggest in a general and tentative way some alternative orientations which, among several possibilities, Christian theism may yet wish to take in days to come.

2.

Contemporary Atheism and Christian Theism

THERE is an old proverb that a good man deserves an enemy to tell him his faults. Perhaps this nugget of folk wisdom might have been a little richer, albeit less euphonious, if besides hoping that even good men would become conscious of their shortcomings, it had managed to stress that a hostile critic is an invaluable aid also in the cultivation of one's truth. It is not, of course, a critic's hostility that counts, but his freedom from prejudice in one's favor and, thereby, his aptness for ferreting out every last weakness in one's position. Indeed, the enemy should be sought in his home ground. It does not infrequently happen that the appreciation of our own truth, the understanding of our own ways and the development of our own experience are uniquely enhanced if we speculatively entertain views contrary to ours, if we pursue our acquaintance with foreign ways, and if we beg to share in someone else's novel experience.

It would not be unreasonable to suppose, therefore, that if a Christian should wish to understand, appreciate and develop the truth of his own theistic belief, he might usefully approach the subject through a consideration of atheism. Or does not the very existence of atheism in the midst of a culture which is historically theistic, a culture which despite its apostasy remains culturally and anthropologically describable in no other terms than Western Christendom, tell us something about the nature of Christian theism? Had modern atheism been imported from abroad the case might be different. But it happens to be a historical fact that our atheism is indigenous. We devised it ourselves, strictly out of our own cultural resources. Evidently, modern atheism is the atheism of the Christian world.

Now, the theism with which we are professedly concerned here is *Christian* theism. But since there are in our modern world varieties of atheism as well as of theism, a comparative approach to the determination of the meaning of specifically Christian theism should direct its attention above all to that atheism which most directly opposes it. We should begin, therefore, with a commonly accepted distinction, first made by Henri de Lubac and subsequently widely reproduced, between "*a*theism, in the strict sense of the word, [and] *anti*theism, or, more precisely, antichristianism."[1]

To find an instance of strict a-theism we would have to turn to someone like Martin Heidegger or, possibly, to Jean-Paul Sartre. I say only *possibly* regarding the latter because of the large element of negativity which often colors his more fundamental and privative dis-belief. Not infrequently Sartre takes the trouble to *deny* the existence of God and to attempt to disprove it. And whoever does so, has by so much departed from a-theism and entered into anti-theism. The denial of the existence of God as an actuality requires the admission of the existence of God as at least a logical possibility—not necessarily, of course, as a real one. For the anti-theist God is, if nothing else, thinkable. For the a-theist he is not.

[1] *The Drama of Atheistic Humanism,* (London, 1949), p. v.

ABSOLUTE ATHEISM

In Heidegger, for example, we meet an atheism which might properly claim not only the name a-theism but indeed *absolute* atheism. This refers to a radical and unconditional commitment to the non-existence—rather, to the impossibility of the existence—of God. But this formula is somewhat misleading. Absolute atheism does not simply affirm the non-existence of God: this would be but the logical converse of the simple negation of the existence of God. What absolute atheism affirms, if it cares to talk about it, is the utter unreality of God. And this can properly take place only in lived existence. It does not admit of discussion, because the idea does not make sense. It could not be argued about by the absolute atheist any more than a madman's ravings could be seriously debated by a sane man. This atheism, which alone deserves the term "a-theism," proceeds from an understanding of being that renders absurd the very possibility of a transcendence that would transcend the transcendence of man. Its consequent dis-belief in God is not like the contemporary chemist's disbelief in the phlogiston, but more like the common man's disbelief in solipsism.

Heidegger's refusal to deny the existence of God, confining himself under persistent questioning to reluctant admissions of the irrelevance of God to philosophical investigation and his absence from life,[2] is grounded on the view that the self and the world are *all* that can be disclosed to consciousness in the phenomenon of existence, *Dasein*. To refer any experience, or

[2] Cf. Thomas Langan, "Heidegger in France," *Modern Schoolman,* XXXIII, January 1956, pp. 115–116; Roger Troisfontaines, *Existentialism and Christian Thought,* (London, 1950), p. 48. But some scholars interpret Heidegger either as a crypto-theist or as a theist *d'intention;* see H. J. Blackham, *Six Existentialist Thinkers,* (London, 1952), p. 103, and Frederick Copleston, *Existentialism and Modern Man,* (London, 1958), p. 18.

any way of being, or any phenomenon, to any reality beyond the *totality* of being is a metaphysical absurdity and a logical contradiction in terms. The hallmark of this unconditional or absolute atheism is its theoretical indifference to theism or, at least, an absence of militancy which would be difficult to reconcile with a certain ostentatiousness one frequently meets in Sartre,[3] or with the passionate scorn one constantly finds in Camus.

The latter was clearly not an a-theist, but an anti-Christian anti-theist, albeit an anti-Christian whose contempt for Christian belief was motivated by a noble and profound devotion to a human truth which, to his mind, Christianity had hopelessly corrupted and totally betrayed. But possibly the most typical, and certainly the most influential, form of anti-Christian atheism (I shall now revert to the common usage and continue to call it *atheism*) is the atheism of Marxism. It is to this atheism that we shall now turn in order to enquire what it might tell us about Christian theism by virtue of its direct opposition to it.

RELATIVE ATHEISM

Marxist atheism is above all a *denial* of the existence of God. This formula is to be understood strictly. It is a negative existential judgment concerning an object of thought, God, who is, therefore, at least by implication, allowed the status of a logically possible, conceivable reality. This is important, because from its negative character it follows that atheism *as such* is not actually the absolutely first metaphysical principle of Marxism. As a negation of a certain existence it rests upon a prior affirmation of another existence. This other existence is not far to seek: it is the existence of man. The denial of God is the logical con-

[3] Cf. Etienne Borne, *Atheism* (New York, 1961), p. 33.

sequence of the affirmation of man, because for Marxism (a) the affirmation of each is held to be incompatible with that of the other, and (b) the existence of man is held to be scientifically, psychologically, logically, physically, metaphysically and, above all, *morally* undeniable. In Marx's own words, "a being does not regard himself as independent unless he is his own master, and he is only his own master when he owes his existence to himself . . . atheism is a *negation of God* and seeks to assert by this negation the *existence of man*."[4] Like every other contemporary atheism, Marxism is therefore a humanism. But unlike absolute and unconditional atheism, Marxist atheism is atheistic because of a prior commitment to humanism, not vice versa. For this reason it must be called *relative* and *conditional*. It is conditioned by its prior commitment to man, and it is relative to a concept of God according to which he is existentially incompatible with man.

Though Marxism has developed in many other respects during the hundred years of its life, in what pertains to its atheism it remains unquestionably bound to its origins. Roger Garaudy, who is surely among the most authoritative living exponents of Marxist-Leninist atheism, makes it evident that his atheism is not of the variety I have called absolute when he quite incidentally mentions that it is conditioned by what he can and cannot conceive God to be like.[5] Likewise, he must be situated well within the central Marxist tradition when he typically defines atheism as "the reducing of the religious fact to the human fact."[6] The implication, as he makes clear else-

[4] *Economic and Philosophic Manuscripts of 1844,* in the T. B. Bottomore edn., *Karl Marx: early writings,* (London, 1963), pp. 165–167. (Italics in the original.) Cf. Karl Marx and Friedrich Engels, *The German Ideology,* (Moscow, 1964), p. 31.

[5] *From Anathema to Dialogue,* (New York, 1966), p. 95.

[6] *Ibid.,* p. 109. Cf. *The German Ideology,* p. 38 *et passim.*

where, is that Marxist atheism in no way should reject whatever true values might be genuinely contained in man's religious experience—all the while insisting, of course, that the casting of any human truth in religious form is at least an imperfection, and oftentimes a perversion, of those true human values. Attention should also be drawn to Garaudy's thought that "one could not [reasonably] conceive a God who would always be in process of making himself, in process of being born," and that man's hunger for totality, absoluteness, mastery of nature and interpersonal reciprocity "is, I think, the flesh of [what the Christian thinks to be] God."[7] M. Garaudy's appeal to reasonableness in one's conception of God shows well the relative character of his disbelief. The question of God bears upon his existence—which is denied on the ground that the conception of God here involved (and, presumably, every other one that has ever been reasonably entertained) does not make sense in the light of the conception of man of which we are immediately conscious. In this view, thus, there *is* a reality behind the conception of God—but this reality is truthfully manifested, purged of absurdity, and thus rendered capable of reasonable existential affirmation, only when its true name is discerned. And that name is not God, but man. This atheism is therefore quite far from that which "follows the route of metaphysical pessimism and tragedy, [for it] would believe itself justified by an optimistic philosophy of science and history. In [Marxist] . . . atheism [the Christian] God is *replaced* by another God."[8]

I have emphasized this characteristic of Marxist atheism

[7] Garaudy, *op. cit.*, p. 95.

[8] Etienne Borne, "Sources et cheminements de l'athéisme," in M. Veuillot, A. M. Henry *et al.*, *L'athéisme: tentation du monde, réveil des chrétiens?*, (Paris, 1963), p. 119. (Italics mine.)

because beyond the immediate purpose of helping us understand certain aspects of Christian theism it should also affect deeply in the practical order the relations of Marxism and Christianity. On the other hand, it would be unprofitable both theoretically and practically, both for Marxism and for Christianity, to leave, even by omission, any doubt on this point: nothing of what I have said above means that Marxism is a crypto-theism or a theism *d'intention*. What I have wished to suggest is that the opposition of Marxist atheism and Christian theism is, though real, by no means an absolute and total contradiction. Moreover, apart from being false, the irenic, if not also syncretistic, idea that Marxism is a theism *d'intention* would be patronizing and insensitive to the scrupulous avoidance of Marxist thinkers, whenever they have dialogued with Christians, of any suggestion that Christian humanism is an atheism unaware of its own nature. And beyond what might be required by comity there is the fact that Marxist humanism, though affirming the transcendence of man towards an absolute, denies the transcendence of the absolute towards man. Of that which man's existence transcends Marxists "can say everything except: It is."[9] At the limit of man's historical consciousness Marxists find no *presence* whatever. Indeed, they find an *absence,* and this is the absence of God.

For all that, to a Christian the ground should at this point begin to appear strangely familiar. The very terminology used by some Marxist atheists to describe the experience of atheism has had an honorable place in certain strains of the best Christian tradition. St. John of the Cross, for example, did not hesitate to refer to his own "experience of the absence of

[9] Garaudy, *op. cit.,* p. 95.

God."[10] But the similarity is more than verbal. To find an *absence,* that is, to find *no presence,* is rather like to find a presence in at least one respect. The *finding* involved in both cases is not at all like an empirical discovery: were either the existence or the non-existence of God a matter of *fact* the issue would be both easily settled and unimportant. In finding either the absence or the presence of God we have to do with a fundamental mode of self- and world-consciousness which is concretized in a radical resolve, that is, in a commitment of oneself, to a certain *projected* existence. One has to decide both whether to believe and whether to dis-believe. Moreover, both Christian theism and Marxist atheism are commitments of one and the same order. I will not say that both are religious commitments if it should give offence to atheists. But perhaps this would not be obnoxious if I stipulated that by *religion* I mean here a mere phenomenological and cultural fact, namely, some sort of fundamental attitude towards totality and resolve towards existence, regardless of the specific content of that attitude. For

> the decision to believe, made with authenticity, appears to have roots other than emotional weakness or monistic prepossessions. The decision to believe springs from a decision about what in human experience is to be taken as the criterion of the real. As each man is, so will he decide what is most real in human experience. According to that decision, he will shape his own identity.[11]

But, of course, the same is true of the decision to dis-believe, because

> belief is opposed to unbelief as one radical interpretation of human destiny to another. . . . The serious nonbeliever and the serious believer share a hidden unity of spirit. When both do all they can to be

[10] *Cántico Espiritual,* Canción I, 16; cf. Canción I, 1–3.
[11] Michael Novak, *Belief and Unbelief,* (New York, 1965), p. 135.

faithful to their understanding and to love, and to the immediate task of diminishing the amount of suffering in the world, the intention of their lives is similar, even though their conceptions of what they are doing are different. Such a unity in the intention of two lives seems in the end to be more profound than a unity on the conceptual level. Some Christians . . . feel closer to non-believers like Albert Camus than to other Christians whom they know, in their understanding of the fundamental dynamism of the human spirit.[12]

In sum, Marxist atheism has certain important points of contact with Christian theism. One is of particular relevance to the purpose at hand: like Christian theism, Marxist atheism, when it is consciously and resolutely embraced, is embraced in an act of faith. In Christian terms we would say that both Christian theism and Marxist atheism are religious commitments. But we might quite as well use other terms and say that both are ultimate existential (and therefore essentially humanistic) commitments. For though Christian belief might be, to a Marxist, an anti-human humanism (just as Marxism might be for a Christian an antireligious religion), Christian belief in God is nevertheless an act of existential self-relation to ultimate reality—and Marxists would not deny that their atheism must be described in precisely the same terms.

Therefore, it matters little for present purposes whether we agree to call the order of reality under discussion the religious or the humanistic. The point is that Marxist atheism and Christian theism differ in content but not in form. In either case we have to do with the order of ultimate self-commitment, ultimate self-disposition towards reality: in either case we have to do with faith. For although the inexistence (just like the existence) of God may well be reasonable, the inexistence (just like the existence) of God is *inevident*. There are, thus, reason-

[12] *Ibid.*, pp. 189, 191.

able "proofs" for the inexistence of God—and there are their counterparts for the existence of God. From this antithesis we may draw, not the skeptical conclusion that no one can decide whether to believe (or dis-believe) that God exists (as if any-one ever waited for the experts to arbitrate the matter and cast his lot with the winning side), but we may observe the verifiable fact that no one (unless he deceives himself) can find such "proofs" remotely sufficient to necessitate a personal commit-ment to existence.[13] Both Marxist atheism and Christian theism are faiths because they are total self-commitments—and *no* total self-commitment, whether towards God, towards man, towards one-self, towards another or towards "things" can ever be any-thing but what Kierkegaard called an existential "leap." More precisely, a faith is a commitment of one's existential self in the light of a certain apprehension of reality as disclosed in lived experience. Marxist atheism and Christian theism are truly op-posed because there is a real difference between them respecting that attitude towards reality and that apprehension of it.

But they are not opposed insofar as they share the same grounds upon which commitment is exercised. This is why Marxist atheism is relative not only in the sense previously explained, but also in the sense that it opposes Christian theism on its own ground. It is, therefore, truly an anti-theism, and specifically and historically an anti-Christian anti-theism. The

[13] I interpret the teaching of Vatican I concerning the demonstrability of God's existence as relative to its preoccupation with fideism. Even among Thomists very few have drawn from St. Thomas, *ST,* II–II, 1, 5, the idea that in point of fact any demonstration can actually replace the Christian's act of faith in God (though some have actually drawn it). At the other extreme, Etienne Gilson puts it a little more strongly than many Thomists when he says that "faith [cannot] be either increased or diminished by acquiring rational certitude or losing it," *Elements of Christian Philosophy,* (New York, 1960), p. 55.

two faiths are not so far apart that they do not conflict. On the contrary, they are sufficiently close to compete for the same allegiances and to stand towards each other as mutually exclusive faiths. If both Christianity and Marxism have long maintained that their welfare, if not also their existence, required the decline, if not also the annihilation, of the other, the reason is not that they have been totally mistaken about each other: the incompatibility is real enough. The reason is that they have perceived only one side of the ambivalent relations that historically and logically bind them in an intimate sado-masochistic embrace. Their mutual exclusion is but the result of their mutual relativity. (A Marxist might say that thesis and antithesis are never too far apart.) To put it lightly: the *whole* difference between Marxist atheism and Christian theism has to do with the existence of God. Surely that makes them somewhat similar faiths. It is not as if they differed concerning the nature of the God they respectively deny and affirm.

But this must be more precisely explained. Marxists sometimes reject a God who is not the Christian God, they reject a God who is rightly to be rejected. Likewise, Christian anti-atheism just as often bears upon crude and contrived caricatures of atheism. At the other extreme, Marxists sometimes squarely reject the true God of the Christian faith. Likewise, some Christians firmly believe in God notwithstanding their appreciation of the reasonableness, legitimacy, viability and morality of an atheistic *religious faith* such as Albert Camus' or Roger Garaudy's. But these two extremes are, if not rare, certainly not representative of the whole sum of relations between Christian theism and Marxist atheism. We can leave aside the unreal, unresolved conflict of prejudiced beliefs at one end, and the real but co-operative mutual dissent of tolerant and mutually respectful faiths at the other. Marxist-Christian relations are better revealed by the far broader spectrum which ranges between the two. I refer now, on the Christian side, to the Christian rejection of the atheism which is genuinely but *unfaithfully* believed in by Marxists. The Marxist counterpart is the rejection of the God who is truly that of the Christian faith, but who in fact is *unfaithfully* believed in by us.

But the range is vast indeed, and I cannot explore its full extent. I will not expand on the Christian anti-theism provoked by the unfaithful atheism of so many Marxisms in power—their inhuman humanism, as it were, of which much could be said—except to suggest that we have to do here with a mutual scandal that calls for better theoretical understanding of atheism on the part of Christians and a more faithful practice of humanism on the part of Marxists. Nor will I expand on the need for reciprocal measures to avoid the other mutual scandal which results when the Christian unfaithfulness to theism—our atheistic theism, as it were—provokes Marxist anti-theism. Much could be said on this too. But we must leave aside all that would involve predominantly moral considerations, the practical unfaithfulness to a faith, Christian or Marxist, that we both already know about, the unfaithfulness of recognized weakness and of repentant or unrepentant shame. What we must dwell upon instead is that which the facts of unfaithfulness to either the Christian or Marxist faith reveal about the nature of that faith: this is what we have not yet begun to face. What are the implications of the unfaithfulness of both Marxists and Christians to their own faiths? I mean, what are the implications of this for an *understanding* of our own Christian or Marxist faith?

I will leave to Marxists the analysis of the latter. We are now entering on a path that an outsider cannot comfortably tread.

I will confine myself to the meaning of unfaithfulness to the Christian faith—I mean, the unfaithfulness that every Christian's true faith *must* suffer. I have in mind the constant, never ending active effort which faith requires under pain of decline, that is, the need for perpetual renewal and growth which corresponds to the faith's always falling short of itself. For belief does not take place in an "act"—even if some moments of one's religious life are more vital than others. For faith is always coming-into-being, it is never quite fully faithful, it is always on the way, hence never perfect and achieved. And if faith is a mode of existence, then Christian theism is a way of life.

ABSOLUTE AND RELATIVE CHRISTIAN THEISMS

If faith were sufficiently well represented by the Scholastic concept of an intellectual assent (under the impulse of the will) to the truth of revealed propositions, the observable fact that faith is found in varying degrees of intensity—varying not only from man to man, and within the same man from time to time, but also in the Church as a whole from age to age—would not be of much importance for an understanding of Christian theism. But it is important if the existential nature (that is, the ontic, "real life" character and not merely the logical and representative nature) of the act of faith is taken account of. Faith is the existential response of the self to the openness of the transcendence disclosed by conscious experience. It is our decision to respect, to let be, the contingency of our being, and, therefore, to admit into our calculations a reality beyond the totality of being. It is a lived response, identical with our freely willing to exist in a certain self-conception and self-resolution; within its unity we can by abstraction distinguish between our openness to the openness of transcendence—to which we often but unnecessarily restrict the meaning of faith—and the return or self-projection of ourselves towards the ultimate transcendence (that is, towards that which lies in the openness of that transcendence which we grasp in consciousness as constituting the "spiritual substance" of man).[14] For the reality of Christian belief is distorted if we understand the "act" of faith as a discrete operation. It is no less a coming-into-being than the "act" of existence which is, likewise, a perpetual achieving of the unachieved. In real life we find not the act, but the *life* of faith.

We cannot believe in God once-for-all any more than we can exist once-for-all. Faith must always realize itself, and yet must always remain unrealized. If so, it must beware of seeking rest if it should feel the fatigue of self-exertion—as must he who, tired of existence, imagined he could find repose outside it. The Scholastic idea that in the beatific vision (a telling expression) faith will be superseded by the "science of the blessed" (another symptomatic coinage) is understandable, given its philosophical and other cultural contexts. But it does not convey the *continuity* of achieving-belief and achieved-belief; like thinking that the achievement of existence is death, this is the kind of idea that would befit Heidegger more than it would Christian faith. Nor is it likely to warn us that to the degree that we cease *believing* and presume to rest on our *belief* we are likely to become unfaithful to our faith. For when we so rest we are tempted to compromise; and finding ease and certitude, the quotidian and the commonplace—possibly even our consolation and reward—in our belief, we are apt to arrest the development of our religious life.

From the nature of the Christian faith thus understood we can

[14] The unity of this existential act enables St. Paul to speak of the "obedience of faith," Rom. 1, 5 (in the RSV, but equivocally rendered "obedience to the faith" in Douay).

derive a conclusion of immediate relevance to Marxist-Christian relations. Like the atheism of Marxists, the theism of Christians is not absolute. It is *relative* and *conditioned*. Indeed, absolute theism would be an infidelity to the Christian faith. It must be considered a temptation to be shunned, a temptation which we have perhaps not altogether managed to avoid at all times.

I have already characterized absolute atheism: it is the belief that nothing could possibly be God. Absolute theism is the belief that anything is apt to be God. But it can take many forms. In primitive man it is manifested in the crude guises of manaism, animism, totemism, polytheism and henotheism. At a much more sophisticated level it becomes the pantheism of, say, the Stoics—from which it can rise to the level of Spinoza's, and finally to the most absolute theism yet devised, namely, that of Hegel, at which point its dialectical equivalence to absolute atheism begins to appear. However, not every absolute theism need take such a pure form as Hegel's or be perfectly consistent with itself. It need not even be pantheistic. It can take the form of the absolute *monotheism* into which Christians can lapse.

Absolute monotheism can be a facile and indiscriminate theism which cares more for belief itself than for the reality, God, to which belief should be merely a way. The absolute theism of Christians can take trivial and even ridiculous forms—as it does when the name of God becomes, precisely as name, an object of worship, so that, for instance, we automatically incline to back almost any domestic or international politician who resorts freely and frequently to the name of God—though we should not underestimate the attrition, the cumulative erosion that religious puerilities can produce. But it is at bottom hardly a matter of words. Our bandying about the name of God—I mean, even in religious, theological, homiletic, catechetical and liturgical discourse—is only a reflection of the recklessness with which we pretend to divine the "will of God," the self-confidence with which we assume that we know the truth about him and can but for the asking share it with any well-disposed mind, and the absence of all embarrassment (if not indeed the presence of a glow) when we confess to each other, and to ourselves, and even to God, that we *do* believe in him.

We might also recall that immoderation in belief which is manifested, for instance, in the unreflecting disposition to err on the side of God, or in the attitude that whatever is "religious" is good, or that whatever is done or proposed on behalf of God is thereby to be given the benefit of the doubt, if any exists. (Are we not *a priori* friendlier to Jung than to Freud, to Maurras than to Blondel, to Hubble than to Hoyle?) This immoderation is possibly also the reason why religious camp and superstitions, too silly to honor by direct mention, continue to proliferate in the Church. They are fertilized by the idea that almost any religion is better than none. They are but symptoms of our readiness of bow before almost anything if it can be suspected of being God. They indicate the facility with which we are satisfied that something or other *is* God. Thus, the one superstition that really matters today is the superstition that only misguided or ignorant individuals can foster superstition, but that "pious beliefs" or practices sanctioned by tradition or by the Church as a whole must therefore be healthy.[15] The non-Christian cannot always be blamed if he is repelled by Christianity's circus games. More to the point, perhaps, might be to blame ourselves if we are not repelled by them.

But moral considerations are irrelevant to present purposes. As

[15] In "A post-Christian age?" *Continuum,* I, 4 (Winter, 1964), 556–567, I have discussed the point less summarily.

weaknesses of individuals or of the Church we could leave all these things aside. But the fact that they happen is important, because they tell us something about the nature of the Christian faith. They need point to no one's guilt. But they do point to the permanent possibility of our not being sufficiently exacting as to the precise meaning of the God that we place our belief in.

The implication of the fact that these failings can occur is that we cannot in good conscience, on account of the nature of the Christian faith, believe indiscriminately; that the Christian faith must be, under pain of idolatry, painstakingly self-critical; that in the Christian tradition, *which* God we believe in is of the utmost importance; and that the Christian faith requires us, under pain of infidelity, to profess *atheism* in relation to every false God. This means that the Christian faith is *both* belief and dis-belief. It requires conscious separation of that in which we must, from that in which we must not, believe. It is this need for critical discrimination that makes the Christian faith essentially unstable, searching and dependent upon constant renewal and development. (It also makes it speculative, as we shall note below.)

This kind of belief can be characterized only as a conditional and relative theism. An unconditional and absolute monotheism would require no more than the affirmation of God pure and simple; it would be an affirmation of something fairly obvious, of something not evocative of questions and basically, therefore, a matter of good sense. A conditional and relative theism, on the other hand, requires not simply care but even suspicion of any falsity, and jealousy towards the truth, of one's conception of God. A relative theism is, in one form or another, agitated and restless—not necessarily with the agitation of worry, not necessarily indeed with the restlessness of speculation, but in any event constantly driven forwards, if not to theorizing to meditation, if not to meditation to proselytism, if not to proselytism to witness, if not to witness to prophecy, if not to prophecy to action, if not to action to the prayer of repose.

Now, the Scholastic distinction between supernatural and natural faith is not highly relevant to contemporary life. But despite its faulty conceptualization, which weds it to an antiquated philosophy of man, it corresponds to a vital reality of Christian life, namely, that the Christian belief in God is quite unlike faith in anything or anyone else. This is manifested in the fact that belief in God does not settle anything about human life. In fact, to the degree that it rules one's life faith is, if anything, *unsettling*. The faith of an absolute theism, on the contrary, does not require constant self-surpassing. It does not imply the *overcoming* of inevidence, even if in point of fact it goes (as commonsense often does) well beyond what is evident. It is true, of course, that Christian *pistis* and Christian *fides* are a *certitude* and a *reliance*. But they are so only *in relation* to the inevidence they affirm. Faith is essentially *relative* to the "things that appear not."[16]

The Christian faith is likewise conditioned by the ultimacy of its personal commitment. It is the sort of decision that so single-mindedly and so exclusively refers one to an-other that it cannot be referred back to oneself: it requires the believer to subordinate his own belief to the reality of God. The Christian cannot believe because he elects to believe. But I am not talking about faith's initiative lying with God's grace, a Scholastic formula which given its assumptions can hardly be gainsaid, (but which puts the matter backwards, beginning as it does with the

[16] Heb. 11, 1.

epistemological view that faith, indeed any experiential or human reality, can be examined and understood from the outside). I am talking about an empirical fact. Reflection on our own belief reveals that the Christian act of faith exhibits this curious feature: concern about the *truth* of belief. That which in a "natural" faith (for example, faith in one's spouse) would be abnormal, undesirable and indicative of a fault (for example, concern, doubt, suspicion, jealousy), in the Christian "supernatural" faith is a condition *sine qua non*. For it would be either pathological or morally wrong if a man's ordinary attitude were one of concern over the truth of his confidence in his wife—yet this concern is *normal* in our belief in God. This, to repeat, is due to the utter and ultimate subordination of the faith itself to the God of Christian belief. We cannot without idolatry believe in anything or anyone else in the same way in which we believe in God.

But let us be precise. Like belief in another human being, the belief in God of primitive religions implies a *belief in the truth* of that belief. This is not what I have described above. I have tried to describe a belief in God which requires *concern with the truth* of that belief. This is why the Christian faith is incompletely described in terms of certitude alone—least of all that certitude which comes from *believing* that one's belief is true. The "certitude" of faith is of the sort that allows, rather, *requires* uncertainty. This does not mean, on the other hand, that faith can be described as a sort of doubt. It means that the Christian faith excludes *belief* in the truth of belief. This is why faith seeks to surpass itself precisely as faith. That is, it seeks what it has not, and insofar as it seeks truth it speculates. In any event, the point is that the Christian is not permitted to have faith in faith: he may have faith only in God.

Probably few Scholastics would wish to disagree with the tenor of this last proposition. Yet, could it be meaningfully affirmed if one conceived faith as providing certainty alone? For the Scholastics, faith cannot entertain doubt and therefore must be a state of certainty. And since this certainty does not come from "knowledge," it must come from the object of faith, God, who cannot deceive or be deceived. Its certainty, thus, comes from God's "authority." But how does an inevident object of faith become authoritative *for us* and, thus, the source of certitude? To say that it becomes authoritative because God takes the initiative in giving us grace is only to compound the circularity. For God can be considered by us to be authoritative only if we *first* believe in God. The theory, however unintentionally, has thus fostered a Christian faith which believes in itself before it believes in God. If it has not quite so successfully fostered a Christian faith without concern for its own truth, the vigilance of the magisterium against any possible inroads by fideism may have had something to do with it, though perhaps only by way of reinforcing the natural inclination of the Catholic believer to retain that concern as an integral part of his faith.

The depth of the Christian faith's concern that it believe only in the true God is well illustrated by the typical disorders to which it is prey, namely, the subordination of the *meaning* of God to the *fact* of his existence.[17] Christianity enjoys the doubtful

[17] A difference between the typical disorders of faith of Catholic and Protestant Christianity should be noted. Catholic Christianity has tended to emphasize if not also to exaggerate the Christian faith's concern with truth. Against the possibility of fideism it has been drawn towards rationalism. But since Luther's reaction to Scholasticism ("*Vernunft ist die höchste Hure*"), Protestant Christianity has tended to do likewise with the Christian faith's relativity to inevidence. Yet, both emphases are components of the Christian tradition. It is possible that the maintenance of bare orthodoxy has not compensated the Church for the disadvantages

distinction of being the only higher religion to have become preoccupied with the existence of God to the extent of having neglected his reality. That it so neglected it is the true meaning of the defection of the working class, the secularization of the culture and the apostasy of science, and it is evident from the history of the Church's attitude to social, political and scientific questions. Christianity indeed is the only religion to have generated religious atheism within itself.

THE OPPOSITION OF THEISM AND ATHEISM

From the relativity of Christian theism we can draw certain comparative conclusions about Christian theism and Marxist atheism. If Christian theism is relative and conditional, its opposition to Marxist atheism is likewise relative and conditioned. For the relativity of Christian theism means that it contains a powerful element of true (albeit relative) atheism. For example, should the Christian theist so unconditionally believe in God that he must in practice prefer the practical atheism of a Christian people "who believe that they believe in God but who in reality deny His existence by each one of their deeds"[18] over a theoretical and relative Marxist atheism? (The question is not academic: it is the problem of Christianity in the face of world revolution.) More generally, should the Christian not stand ready to prefer the *relative* atheism of Marxism over an *absolute* Christian theism, that is, a theism which under the guise of Christianity would hide an admixture of paganism?

I am inclined to answer *no* to the first question and *yes* to the

---

of lopsided emphases. From this we may derive the moral that the maintenance of orthodoxy is no criterion of the sufficiency and adequacy of the authoritative (or other) teaching of the Church. Cf. below, p. 128.

[18] Jacques Maritain, "On the meaning of contemporary atheism," *Review of Politics,* II, 3 (July, 1949), p. 267.

second, for two reasons which do not of themselves have to do with moral considerations, but strictly with the nature of Christian theism.[19] First, Christian belief includes a certain atheism—relative, but properly so-called—with respect to certain gods which it cannot tolerate: "with regard to [those gods] the saint is a perfect atheist."[20] Several writers have in recent times recalled that the charge of atheism was frequently levelled at early Christianity, and that the validity of the accusation—relative to a certain understanding of God—was readily acknowledged by Christians, for instance by Justin: "We are called atheists. And yes, we confess it, we are the atheists of those so-called gods."[21]

At a deeper level, Christian belief implies a certain *conditional* dis-belief in God which is merely the obverse of concern for the truth of belief. A genuine and lived concern with truth means a hypothetical willingness to disbelieve should the truth require one to do so. Unconditional belief would mean for the Christian an inordinate attachment to belief, a possibly culpable regard for the returns of his belief—not least likely of all, perhaps, the possible comforts, security and other this- and other-worldly benefits of faith. And yet, the Christian, evidently, must not so dishonestly or pragmatically believe that he would stand ready to continue believing even if he should no longer experience his belief as true. Could he wish that if his belief were false he should never find out? This would be believing for the sake of believing or for the sake of whatever consequences—other than truth—belief may bring. Should we not, on the contrary, believe only because of the truth? Of course, if one's religious experience is predominantly composed of anxiety about going to heaven,

[19] I have dealt with the political-ethical reasons for the same answers in *Christianity and Revolution,* (New York, 1963).

[20] Maritain, art. cit., p. 275.

[21] *I Apologia,* 6, 1.

and if it is suffused with that spiritual hedonism which is above all concerned with the safety of one's immortal soul, the answer to this question may not seem obvious. It may not even seem particularly important.

Thus, belief in the *true God* means not simply belief in a god which, (logically enough), we must *presuppose* to be true, under pain of otherwise not being able to believe at all. It means belief in God precisely *as true*. It would not be inexact, therefore, to say that belief in God really means to have an ultimate commitment to the truth; I mean, to all truth, totally and universally—not particularly to a transcendent, subsistent Truth, that is, not to the presumed Truth of God's self-identity, which is a hellenization of the Christian experience, but to the transcendent truth which is immanent and manifested in every truth. I am talking about the truth which evokes the attitudes of honesty and truthfulness—I mean, that precise sort of openness which is apt to earn self-respect. I refer to that truth which calls for fidelity to the truth wherever and whatever it might be.[22] Religious *dishonesty,* the disposition to advance the cause of God through insincerity, uncandidness, lack of forthrightness (if not through outright deception, both of others and of ourselves), is one of the consequences of disregarding the need to condition the Christian faith in God upon the truth. Conversely, the hallmark of the commitment to God *as true* is a certain conditioning of one's belief by the willingness to admit the real possibility of disbelief—both by another and by oneself.[23]

[22] Signally among modern Catholic philosophers, Gabriel Marcel has emphasized the religious significance of everyday truth; cf. *The Mystery of Being,* vol. 1, (London, 1950), pp. 57–76.

[23] Other aspects of the Christian admission of the possibility of disbelief have been explored by Eugene Fontinell, "Reflections on faith and metaphysics," *Cross Currents,* XVI, 1 (Winter, 1966), 15–40.

Now, if we admit the real possibility of disbelief by another we have discovered the foundation of the Christian tolerance of Marxist atheism, namely, that it is both a reasonable and a moral possibility. And if we admit the possibility of disbelief by ourselves we have discovered the foundation of the reasonableness of the Christian faith—on which is grounded the moral claim of Christian theism to toleration by Marxism. In any event, I have already alluded to the historical fact that atheism as a cultural phenomenon is indigenous to Christian societies. I now recall it in confirmation of the conditional nature of Christian belief and its relativity to disbelief. None but Christian cultures have ever generated atheism, and it is difficult to suppose that any others could have done so. In the Judaeo-Christian tradition, on the contrary, the steady purification of the concept of God has increasingly facilitated the emergence of that peculiar disbelief which, being born of the same religious experience as belief, can fairly be called—in contradistinction to the atheism born of inconsiderateness, unreflectiveness, inexperience, or sheer obstinacy in refusing to admit the possibility of God—*religious atheism*. Does this not tell us something about the nature of Christian theism?

We may indeed conclude that the relative and conditional atheism of Christianity is the obverse of its relative and conditional theism. There is, of course, an important and irreducible difference between Christianity and Marxism despite the fact that both share a relative atheism. For their relative atheisms differ. That of Marxism is relative to its humanism; that of Christianity is relative to its theism. This is why Marxism finds in the human experience of existence the *absence* of God, whereas Christianity finds in the same experience *both* the absence and the presence of God.

From the relative nature of Christian theism follows its aptitude for development, readjustment and cultural polymorphism. It is not given once for all. It is, therefore, dynamic, evolving and self-transforming. But how could Christian theism be all these things and nevertheless *true?* That is, how could it be these things and yet remain, both *originally* and *ever,* a true doctrine of the Christian faith? The answer depends on whether a theory of the development of Christian doctrine could reconcile these apparently contradictory, mutually exclusive qualities of Christian belief.

3.
The Development of Christian Dogma

No responsible Catholic would seriously maintain today that Christian dogma does not, in some sense of the word, develop. But precisely in what sense? This is another question, on the answer to which Catholic thinkers are scarcely unanimous.

It is interesting to note that Catholic theology has only gradually become aware of the fact that dogma develops. St. Thomas was aware that "the articles of faith have increased in the course of time." But this hardly constituted a true development of what is believed: "as regards the substance of the articles of faith, they have not received any increase as time went on, since whatever those who lived later have believed, was contained, albeit implicitly, in the faith of those Fathers who preceded them. But there was an increase in the number of articles believed explicitly, since to those who lived in later times some were known explicitly which were not known explicitly by those who lived before them."[1] The implication here is that doctrine and belief are related, respectively, as objective and subjective realities and are therefore really, entitatively distinct. The articles of faith increase ***in number*** because

[1] *ST,* II–II, 1, 7.

it is possible to express *the same objective dogma,* the same eternal and divine truth, in more explicit and thus *in more complex human terms.* The sense is, however, that the dogma itself does not in any real sense change, although its articulation becomes more complex.

There appears to have been relatively little departure from this fundamental understanding of the matter during the later middle ages.[2] When Bossuet in the seventeenth century contrasted the immutability of Catholic doctrine with Protestant variability, he may have been emphasizing an aspect of the Thomistic doctrine in which St. Thomas took little interest, but he was hardly departing from the common position of mediaeval theology. However, in more recent times,[3] and especially since Newman's *Essay on the Development of Christian Doctrine* (1845), dissatisfaction with this view has increased. The gradual conviction has arisen that Christian dogma must be said *in some real sense* to develop and, indeed, to have been developing since earliest times.

CONSCIOUSNESS AND DEVELOPMENT

I underscore this: the fact of which we have recently become aware is not that Christian doctrine has begun to develop in recent times, but that it has *always* existed in a process of development. It is only the awareness of this fact that is new. This bears emphasis because it serves to raise this question: Why should Christianity at a certain point of its history, and not before, have become aware of a fact about itself which had always been

[2] Fidel G. Martínez, *Evolución del Dogma y Regla de la Fé,* (Madrid, 1962), pp. 96–201.

[3] Cf. Owen Chadwick, *From Bossuet to Newman: the idea of doctrinal development,* (Cambridge, 1957).

so? Why should the Church at a certain point in the history of dogma have become aware that its dogma had a history? When we pose the question in this way the answer immediately suggests itself. The *post-facto* awareness of one's development is not peculiar to Christianity: it is a property of human nature. It can be no coincidence that Christianity reached this awareness concerning itself at the same time that mankind reached the same awareness of its own historicity and its evolutionary nature in every other respect. It is because human experience in general has become aware of its historical character that Christianity has become aware of its own. As man has become historically minded —as he has learned that time is not a reality external to him in relation to which he endures, but rather an essential constituent of his own reality—man has found the understanding of his past history indispensable for the understanding of his present reality and for the adequacy of his self-projection into the future. Christianity has simply shared in this human experience—thus receiving immediate confirmation of its historical nature in the very fact that its religious experience follows the same rules as all human experience. For Christianity, as it has discovered that in point of fact it develops, has by that very fact become aware of its human reality—and at least partly the source of this awareness has been man's growth in the awareness of his own nature.

It is useful to note this, because it provides a valuable premise in the further understanding of the nature of doctrinal development. The preceding considerations mean that Christianity's awareness of the fact that it develops historically must in some sense find its explanation in the nature of human consciousness.[4]

[4] I do not mean that we must find the explanation in exclusively "natural" causes. In the Church's growing awareness of its own nature the Christian faith can see a concrete and wondrous instance of the Holy

Conversely, an understanding of the nature of consciousness facilitates an understanding of the processes behind the fact that Christianity develops historically. When then, in this context, is meant by consciousness?

In contemporary thought (if abstraction is made from the differences of sects and schools), consciousness is understood as the typical and proper form of human psychism—indeed, of human existence and life. Man's psychic life (and he has no other) is distinguished from animal psychism in a much more radical manner than in the philosophical tradition that runs from early Greece to early modern times. According to the most common teaching of the latter tradition, the psychism of the animal consists in the intentional appropriation ("intussusception") of beings other than itself (cognition), and in the correlative intentional self-disposition of itself towards beings other than itself (appetition). It consists, more generally, in effecting an intentional unilateral union of one being (the subject) with another (the object), whether cognitively or affectively. But in the understanding of recent philosophical thought, man's psychic life, however, exhibits a peculiar character which animals do not appear even in part to share. For man is the being who is present to himself. This presence of his being to himself is called *consciousness.*

Both man and animal "know." But the real difference between the two is not that man enjoys to a higher degree, or in a higher mode, the faculty of uniting to himself (intentionally and unilaterally) other beings—for example, by unilaterally grasping an intelligible object immaterially, instead of a merely sensible

---

Spirit's presence in the Church. But this "supernatural" cause has for its effect the Church's heightened *self*-awareness, and increased consciousness of its own nature.

one materially. The difference transcends the order of mere knowledge altogether. Though both man and animal know, that is, intentionally appropriate another being by some form of objectification (which itself may differ widely between man and animal), man's psychism extends beyond knowledge and reaches the level of consciousness. For knowledge, the establishment of intentional relations with another, provides man with the possibility of establishing intentional relations with (that is, knowing) the being of the being that he himself is. This means: man can know not only beings, but be-ing; not only being-as-other, but also being-itself. He can not only become "the other as other" (*aliud in quantum aliud*), but also be other as himself. Thus, the basic characteristic of human existence (revealed by the fact that, being conscious, man is the being, as it were, whose being is outside himself) is sometimes called *transcendence*.

However, the transcendence of man, the nature of consciousness, and man's radical distinction from the animal, would be mistakenly expressed in the formula "Man not only knows, but knows that he knows." For the point is not that man, who can know beings other than himself, can *also* be an object of knowledge for himself. It is not that man can "reflect," that is, make his own (previous) act of knowledge the object of a (new) act of knowledge, and thus know that he is a knower. The point is that in the very act of knowing an object (whether a being other than himself, or the being which is himself) he becomes present to himself. Man does not require a further act of re-flexion in order to be conscious. From the outset of consciousness he is *already* present to his own being. The animal's being, on the other hand, is neither in a first or in a reflective act present to itself—though, to be sure, an animal, if its cognitive apparatus is sufficiently well developed, may well be capable of knowing itself, whether by sensing itself, by proprioception, or perhaps even by knowing some of its own psychic operations. The last would constitute a re-flexion properly so called, since the awareness of that object which, as it so happens, is the subject itself, would take place by means of a psychic act which, if not in time at least in nature, is subsequent to the original psychic act which provides the objection of *reflection.* Man's consciousness, on the other hand, though it objectifies the self in the same manner as it objectifies the non-self, gives us an awareness of a being which does not merely *happen* to be a self; rather, what is typical of it is that it produces this experience: *myself,* that is, *my self's be-ing.* For, to be sure, I know myself as an object. But if I am conscious I know myself as a unique and peculiar object, namely, as be-ing myself. What gives this "object" its uniqueness and peculiarity is this: that it is not an object at all. It is not known as "other." The most basic doubt that cannot possibly be entertained (not merely in good logic, as with Descartes' impossibility of doubting that *I think*—but even in lived experience) is the doubt that I might be an-other. The fundamental empirical (and not merely logical) fact of philosophy is not *cogito,* but *sum.*[5]

The transcendence of man's psychic life, its surpassing of mere knowledge, accounts for the transcendence of human development over that of the animal. The animal develops by learning (in the strict sense of the word), that is, by increasing his knowledge, by knowing *more.* This follows from the cognitive form

[5] Indeed, not merely *sum,* but *sursum,* as Gabriel Marcel remarks; cf. *Homo Viator,* (New York, 1962), p. 26. The same fact with but slightly different emphases could be formulated in other ways. *Cogito* may be accepted if it means not *I think* but *I am conscious;* or better still, *consciousness* (*exists*), in order to signify that the self is not a Cartesian, Kantian or Hegelian transcendent *ego* originally isolated from the world and underlying the mind's awareness of the world.

of its psychic life. Since the perfection of animal life lies in its intentional appropriation of another to itself, and in its intentional self-disposition towards another—or, again, in its intentional unilateral union (cognitive or affective) with another—animal development can only consist in an increase in intentional unilateral union with others, whether by knowing and desiring more and more things, or by knowing and desiring more and more about the same thing. On the other hand, the typical form of human development can only be an increase in consciousness. Its distinctiveness over learning properly so called is that it cannot take the form of a quantitative increase. If consciousness is not the re-flexive knowledge of an object (ourselves, or knowledge itself), but the presence of being to itself, it follows that consciousness cannot develop by quantitative increase (for example, by multiplying the objectification of the same object of consciousness), since the supposed object of knowledge is already present as a whole in the first moment of consciousness. Or, more precisely, man can develop in this way, that is, he can learn, since he can know—in the sense that consciousness virtually contains knowledge. But this is not what defines his human development. For that matter, he also develops physiologically, since physiological life is virtually contained in his psychic existence. But it would be hardly correct to reduce man's development to increased physiological organization and efficiency.

As experience reveals, consciousness develops in a *sui generis* way which we might figuratively describe as *intensification*. Any examples, since drawn from human experience, will of necessity argue circularly. As a light burns more brightly, without changing color, when a rheostat is turned, or as a broadcast is more clearly understood when one raises the volume of the same sound which at first was but with difficulty perceived, growth in consciousness typically comports the experience of knowing clearly now that which, as we "come to think of it," we had been aware of all along, even before we "reflected" on it, and yet had somehow managed not to notice. Consciousness develops as we become conscious of that which, in a sense, we already were conscious of. But this is not a tautology. It means that to heighten one's consciousness is to "realize" that which had been "before our eyes" all the time and which, indeed, we had already seen, but which we now see all over again "in a new light," that is, with a sharper, clearer, heightened or nobler meaning. This new meaning, moreover, is not a substitute for the earlier one. It is possible only insofar as it *emerges from* the earlier one, which it incorporates to itself and brings along with itself into a "fuller" and "richer" experience. The heightening of consciousness presupposes a genuine but *more primitive* consciousness; it can only grow out of it, and it is *meaningful* only in relation to it.

What does this mean for the Christian's understanding of doctrinal development? It means that we can begin to understand not only that, in fact, Christianity develops, but also the reasons why it develops and the anthropological mechanism of its development. The understanding of man's psychic life in terms of consciousness, rather than knowledge, creates the possibility of understanding the truth of the Christian faith in such a way as would not only permit true development to occur, but indeed as requiring it by its very nature as truth. For, to begin with, this truth need no longer be understood as an essentially constant, and substantially immutable, though accidentally variable, relation to an immutable object objectively presented to the Christian intellect.

TRUTH AND DEVELOPMENT

As long as the only concept of man which philosophy has made available to Christian speculation has been some variation of the idea that man is a rational animal—that is, an animal whose distinctiveness lies in the peculiar (that is, intellectual-rational) way in which he intentionally appropriates objects and unilaterally unites them to himself—Christianity has been logically bound to understand its own truth in the same way as it has understood every other truth, namely, as guaranteed by some form of substantial immutability.[6] As long as man's psychic life has been understood as a form of knowledge (upon the specific nature of which free volition follows as an executive power), faith likewise has been understood as a form of actualization of man's intellectual powers (upon the specific nature of which "good works" follow as the execution or "application" of the faith). If so, the truth of man's faith must be correspondingly conceived as the natural relation of conformity of the human intellect to its object—however true it may also be that in the case of faith the intellect's act attains a supernatural and inevident object (under the influence, therefore, of supernatural factors which provide the substitute for evidence).

In this view, which is the traditional one of Scholasticism, although the intellect's *act of faith* differs from the intellect's *act*

[6] For brevity's sake I omit the distinctions and qualifications which the traditional theories of truth rightly insist upon, for example St. Thomas, *De Veritate,* 1, 4–6, where it is explained "how truth changes and how it does not." For, as common sense recognizes, the truth of knowledge must change even as the *things* to which the mind is related change. Insofar as it pertains to mutable things, truth requires constancy of proportion rather than strict immutability. Nevertheless, in this view truth is radically immutable insofar as it amounts to the self-identity of the mind's conformity to a self-identical *object* of thought.

of knowledge (properly so called), the *truth* of the act of faith is of the same nature as the *truth* of any natural act of the intellect. This may well be one source of the fairly common assumption that the notion of Christian truth as eternal and immutable is an integral part of the Christian faith. Rather, it would be better to say that, since an integral part of the Christian faith is the affirmation that it is true, then, as long as one conceives truth (whether at the level of common sense or that of philosophical enquiry) as an essentially immutable and invariable relation of mind to its object, one must interpret accordingly the truth of faith. In other words, *if* the Scholastic theory of truth is correct, then Christian truth is eternal and immutable. But this scarcely compels one to conclude that to diverge from the Scholastic conception of truth is to diverge from the truth of faith. Since there is, so far as I understand the matter, no revealed Christian theory of truth, any theory of truth used or assumed by Christian teaching or speculation must run the same risks and be subject to the same development as, say, a cosmological or anthropological theory used or assumed by them.

Now, the Scholastic doctrine is as follows. If the truth of faith is of precisely the same nature as that of knowledge, namely, the correspondence[7] of the intellect to its object, it follows that the

[7] Thomists sometimes object to the word *correspondence* on the grounds that nowadays it may tend to connote "one-to-one correspondence," whereas in St. Thomas's doctrine the correspondence is one of proportion or ad-equation. Nevertheless, the meaning of the terms used by St. Thomas, *convenientia, correspondentia, adaequatio,* and *conformitas* (*De Veritate,* I, 1) is clear. We have to do with *two* beings, knower and known, and truth is a relation of the knower to the known precisely insofar as the two are ontologically *separated* but intentionally *united* in the knower's intentional possession of the known, and this relation consists in the *sameness* (possibly a partial sameness, since things are not usually known exhaustively), or *likeness* of the knower-in-act (of knowing) and the known-in-act (of being known), that is, the knower as such and the known as such.

truth of faith can develop in precisely the same way as that of knowledge and in no other way. It can develop only within the limitations imposed by the nature of truth. For example, faith can, like knowledge, grow as a virtue. Just as the wise man has greater knowledge when he can more easily posit acts of knowledge due to a more perfect habit of knowledge,[8] faith can develop in the sense that the believer can have more perfectly, more intensely, the habit of faith. Moreover, faith can develop in another way, namely, respecting the contents it possesses, precisely as possessed. This means: faith can develop insofar as it produces an effect upon the intellect, namely, the intellect's possession of objects *as such*. It can develop in respect of that which is attained insofar as it is *attained* (object), but not insofar as it *is* (thing, *res*).[9] Therefore, it can develop in two ways, for man's knowledge can grow in respect of what is known (not insofar as it is, but insofar as it is known, that is, possessed or objectified), in two ways.

Knowledge can increase, first, in the sense that man can know objects of knowledge previously unknown to him. This is, of course, not an increase in the knowledge he already has, but an increase in the total amount of knowledge he possesses at a later time. Knowledge is thus said to increase in the sense that the mind assimilates *new* objects of knowledge. But knowledge can also increase in a second way, namely, in the sense that man can know better that which he already knows. How does this happen? It happens when an object of knowledge which at first is known simply, becomes known later in a complex way, that is, according to the multiplicity of concepts in which it can be

[8] *ST,* I–II, 52, 2.
[9] *ST,* III, 12, 2.

analyzed.[10] In other words, to know a thing better means to know *more things* about the same thing.

The Christian faith taught by the Church (that is, dogma) does not develop in the first way, that is, by the assimilation of new objects of faith—though the faith of the individual may be said, in a restricted sense of the term, so to develop. For instance, an individual might well believe one truth of faith without having so much as heard of another (though his faith in the first implicitly contains his faith in the other). But in the absence of new revelation after the close of the New Testament era, the faith of Christianity cannot teach any *new* truths. In the past, of course, as God's revelation took place over a long period of time, new truths (the Trinity, the Incarnation) were revealed and taught, pre-eminently by Christianity in relation to Judaism. But once revelation was complete, the articles of the faith taught by Christianity could only increase in the second way, namely, by the explicitation of objects of intellectual assent implicitly contained in prior objects of faith. It is clear that this kind of development does not contradict the stability of the truth of faith. As we have seen, it means that "as regards the substance of the articles of faith, they have not received an increase."

On the assumption, apparently, of some such understanding of the matter, a fairly recent decree of the Inquisition (as the Holy Office was then still known), condemned the proposition that "the chief articles of the Apostles' Creed did not have the same sense for the Christians of the first ages as they have for the

[10] I have abstracted here, for the sake of brevity, from the fact that according to Scholasticism knowledge can increase both analytically and synthetically, so that knowledge of what is simpler, first, and more knowable in itself, is not necessarily known simply or first by us, and is not necessarily more knowable to us.

Christians of our time."[11] If Christian dogma can develop in no deeper sense of the word than that admitted by St. Thomas, the position reflected by this decree must necessarily follow—precisely because it means that dogma does not develop *at all*. This sort of "development" would by definition preclude the appearance of not only those new doctrines which would either contradict or be unaffiliated with the original doctrines; it would also preclude the appearance of any novelty whatever. Even as to the sense it has *for us* every doctrine must be reducible to identically the same sense as the original. If we called this "development" we would be using the word in other than its common contemporary acceptation. The assumption which underlies this view is that any novelty not *totally* reducible to the original would imply a substantial divergence from—and thus a corruption of —the original. If the original object of the Christian faith was true, any novelty (other than that of the mere explicitation of "the same sense" of that which "was contained, albeit implicitly, in the faith of the Fathers"), must be false. Conversely, any novelty not so reducible could be true only if the original faith was false.

On what grounds could exception be taken to this position? Principally on two. First, this doctrine assumes that the human experience within which Christian belief occurs has not changed between the days of the early Church and our own—and this assumption must be judged as contrary to fact. Second, it ignores many indications that there may be something in the nature of man, in the nature of experience, in the nature of truth, and possibly even in the nature of the Christian faith, that impels man to look ever deeper into the truth and indeed, to be dissatisfied with the very truth of what he holds to be true.

[11] *Lamentabili Sane,* (July 3, 1907), Proposition 62, (DS 3462).

In this connection it may be pertinent to recall that the Reformation's anti-Roman character was rendered possible by the Reformers' assumption of basically the same idea concerning the fixity of Christian doctrine. But assuming also the premise that the contemporary Church, under the Roman pontificate, *had* substantially changed the original sense, the Reformers had to conclude that Christianity had been corrupted, and that the Christian faith must regain its original primitive sense. It would be unfortunate if, as more and more Catholics find it impossible to reconcile the historicity of human nature with Proposition 62 of *Lamentabili,* they should draw a conclusion paradoxically similar to that of the Reformers, and looked backwards to the original "purity" of "traditional" Christianity instead of forward to the demands of the future. It is possible that loyalty to the Catholic Church would be best safeguarded by a theory of dogmatic development which, faced with a choice between Proposition 62 and the facts of experience and history, would not necessarily opt for the first—in other words, by a theory of development that would integrate contemporary experience and faith.

CONSCIOUSNESS AND TRUTH

If we understand man's intellectual life to be not a subject's assimilation of objects to itself (and of itself to objects), but the emergence of a self as it becomes present to itself by self-differentiating itself from the totality of being, then we should understand human psychism not as the operation of a faculty of a substance which would alone exercise primary existence, but as a reality which constitutes the very being of man. If so, man's psychic life is not the mind's (unilateral and intentional) *union* with a reality from which it was originally separated by its substantive self-containment. On the contrary, it is the mind's self-*differentiation* of its-self out of a reality with which it was originally continuous and united in un-differentiation. Consciousness is a process, not in the sense that it is a succession of mental states, but in the sense that it is the function or activity whereby the being of man emerges.

Consciousness develops, therefore, not as an additional perfection of a faculty of a being, a perfection which it gains supererogatorily (as if it did not have to obtain it in order to be, but merely in order to be more perfectly). Consciousness develops, rather, because it is in its nature to develop; unless it developed it would not exist at all. Its motto, as Marcel has said, is not *sum,* but *sursum*. This should serve to emphasize again that consciousness is not the *becoming* (that is, the mental activity) of a *being* (that is, mind, soul or man). It is the coming-into-being of mind, soul and man. There is no real difference, therefore, between the development of *consciousness* and the development of *self-consciousness*. Consciousness cannot be (or, which is the same, cannot develop) unless by the continuous differentiation of the self from objects, so that the heightening of self-consciousness necessarily involves an increase in the "number" of objects known —quite as in the philosophical tradition described above. But neither can consciousness be—rather, come-into-being—unless the presence of being to itself, which constitutes the self, be rendered ever more conscious.

It follows then, if truth is the relation of man's intellectual life to his world, and if that relation is not established in the act of a faculty of man, but in the very constitution of man's being (in the very constitution of his "substance," as we might somewhat equivocally put it), that truth cannot be a mental faculty's conformity to things. The alternative is to conceive truth not as a reality of the order of accidental being, but of the order of "substantial" existence. Truth is not the adequacy of our representative operations, but the adequacy of our conscious existence. More precisely, it is the fidelity of consciousness to being.

This has a twofold meaning. It means, first, the fidelity of consciousness to man's own being, that is, the degree to which the development of consciousness actually occurs and, therefore, the degree to which man comes into being or develops in being. This is why there is always at least some truth in all knowledge.[12] But since consciousness differentiates the self out of the

[12] This is a fact which Scholasticism recognizes (cf. *ST,* II–II, 172, 6), but which it cannot satisfactorily explain. Maritain, for instance, is inconsistent with his own Thomistic doctrine that truth is found only in the judgment, when he explains that a proposition can be "an absolute error," while nevertheless "all the elements that make up this false thought are not therefore false," *Introduction Générale a la Philosophie,* (Paris, 1946), p. 129. For the "elements" that make up the thought are, of course, objects of simple apprehension.

We can discover in what sense some truth is found in a false judgment if we consider the judgment not merely as a logical, timeless entity, but as an ontic, historical one. If so, the judgment in question must be evaluated in the light of the temporality of the enquiry or of the consciousness-development which produced it. Its truth is given to it, as is its falsity, by its historical character. No matter how false, it normally represents a development over a more primitive stage of consciousness. Conversely, falsity is existentially real, it is no mere logical fact. It is necessarily connected with all knowledge, at very least as a real possibility which might in the future be realized. This is why, irrespective of the real truth of knowledge, the reality of error forbids us (not only logically, but ontically, as a matter of good sense and empirical prudence) from making the following judgment—until, if ever, human consciousness evolves into a qualitatively different form: "my knowledge is so true that I cannot conceive the possibility that in the future I should change my mind."

The *reality* of error is not adequately recognized by Scholasticism. The thesis might be developed that Thomistic epistemology cannot in the last analysis account for it. St. Thomas (*De Veritate,* I, 12) states that "the intellect is always true in knowing what a thing is . . . By accident, how-

totality of undifferentiated reality, the faithful, steadfast and continued development of the self can actually occur only to the degree that the world is objectified, that is, conceptualized, systematized, organized, *lived with* and *made meaningful* for our consciousness. In both senses, thus, truth is a quality of man's intellectual life. And in either sense it cannot be maintained except through the heightening of consciousness. It cannot be so much as *retained* unless it grows. For it is not the result of the mind's "inner," reduplicative, intentional reflection of an object "outside" it. It is the result of the mind coming-into-being through the self-differentiation of that-which-is into self and world.

It is true, therefore, that the truth does not depend on man's arbitrary decision to make objects conform to the mind's affirmation of them regardless of what they may be "in themselves." The absurdity of this supposition is evident from the fact that *ex hypothesi* it requires that things be "in themselves" independently of what they may be "made to be" by our arbitrary decisions.

ever, falsity can occur in this knowing of quiddities, if the intellect falsely joins and separates." Of course, if truth is found "in an act of the intellect joining and separating, rather than in an act by which it forms the quiddities of things," (I, 3), it follows that falsity occurs "if the intellect falsely joins and separates." In other words, error is the opposite of truth. But St. Thomas nowhere explains how it is possible for the intellect falsely to "join and separate," nor what accounts for the fact that sometimes it "joins and separates" truly and other times falsely. Assuming the reality of error as the converse of truth, he merely classifies the various ways in which "the intellect falsely joins and separates." Accordingly, the possibility that error has an essential role to play in the emergence, formation and development of truth has not been considered by later Scholasticism. The contemporary human experience, however, is manifested (if badly conceptualized) by the conviction that the human intellect has the "freedom to err." In "Academic freedom and Catholic dissent," *Commonweal,* LXXX, 2 (April 3, 1964), 33–36, I have suggested that this "freedom" should be justified not as the moral right of the individual but on the grounds that error benefits the truth.

This idea of truth is a crude self-contradiction that could not be seriously considered in philosophy for a moment. But it would be equally mistaken to suppose that since this cannot be, the opposite must be true, and that truth depends upon an external reality's *fiat* to the effect that the mind must conform to its requirements regardless of what the mind may need by its nature for its own existence and being.

The long history of philosophy has shown that this concept of truth is in the last analysis equally, though much less obviously, absurd. It would not be so deviously absurd if it could be immediately maintained that the *agent* responsible for knowledge were some "external reality." (Aristotle's immediate successors, like Averroës later, were drawn to just this position.) But if, as St. Thomas resolutely maintained, there cannot be a single "agent intellect" for all men, and the knower himself must be the efficient cause of his knowledge, true knowledge has to bear the impossible, twofold burden of (a) assimilating to the self an-other which, *prior* to knowledge is totally *unrelated* to the self, and (b) ensuring that this assimilation comply with a condition (namely, the *relation* of conformity to the other) established *prior* to knowledge. (Is it not—in retrospect—obvious that, if so, only God could "pre-establish the harmony" of a truth-relation between essentially unrelated objects and subjects?) Conversely, to the degree that early modern philosophy pursued the Greco-medieval theories of knowledge to their bitter end, and in particular the idea that the receptive truth (of human knowledge) must rest upon the truth (of things) actively caused by God's creative knowledge,[13] it became necessary once again to transfer to God the efficient causality of human knowledge. (And ultimately, if the causality, also the content, for example

[13] St. Thomas, *De Veritate,* I, 4.

Malebranche, Gioberti, Rosmini.) For if the truth of human knowledge is to depend upon an external reality's *fiat* which commands the mind's conformity to things, it is more reasonable to specify that it should be the *fiat* of that external reality which is God, rather than the *fiat* of that external reality which is the world around us. It was Descartes, of course, who first began to draw this implication from Scholasticism.

Thus, the conception of truth as a relation of conformity is deficient not only because it is based upon a supposition contrary to both logic and observation (namely, that we can conceive and understand knowledge from the outside, as if we could witness from a third, "higher" viewpoint, the union of two lower things, object and subject). It is also deficient in that it leads to impossible conclusions, principally the denial of the possibility of truth. The notion of the stability of truth leads to its annihilation. On the other hand, the understanding of man's psychic life in terms of consciousness suggests a conception of truth in which substantial transformation of man's understanding of being does not necessarily imply unfaithfulness to an earlier, less well-developed stage of understanding. On the contrary, the normal course of man's intellectual life would require that whatever truth he may acquire be continuously surpassed. For the truth is the *valuable* quality that it is, only because it is part of the process of man's self-creation and coming-into-being.

Perhaps it should be underlined that the deficiency of the traditional conception of truth does not lie in its being a *relation to another*. It lies in the contradiction of making this relation towards another (a) a relation of conformity to the other and, at the same time, (b) a relation unilaterally effected by, and unilaterally existing in, the knower alone. Now, the truth of knowledge *is* unilaterally effected and unilaterally enjoyed by the knower. Therefore, it can be a relation towards being only if it is a *fidelity* rather than a *conformity*. What is the difference between the two? *Conformity* is a relation towards another which is owing to another by reason of the other's nature. *Fidelity* is a relation towards another which one owes to oneself by reason of one's own nature. Conformity obligates from the outside. Fidelity, like nobility, obligates from within.

DEVELOPMENT AND DOGMA

If we conceive faith as consciousness of the background against which human transcendence reveals itself,[14] then we may understand how there could be a development of faith; I mean, not only an intensification of faith as a subjective disposition, but also an intensification of the *truth* of the doctrines of faith.

If this type of development is possible, it should perhaps be fittingly called *progressive,* with all the value connotations attached to the term. For a development of the doctrines of faith as a mere explicitation of the implicit would not be *intrinsically* valuable. It might have some value insofar as purely extrinsic conditions—for instance, the appearance of heresy—would require such explicitation in order to achieve essentially the *same* effect which originally accrued to the earlier faith, namely, a certain conformity between man's intellect and the objects of faith proposed by revelation. However, in the alternative concept development would be desirable in itself, insofar as it would

[14] That is, if we understand it as man's standing in, and acceptance of, the openness revealed by his own transcendence, an acceptance of a fact which he, as it were, confirms, *positively* lets be and allows—in the sense that he commits himself to exist in the presence of this openness despite his inability to comprehend and fill up the totality of transcendence.

mark the intensification of the relation between man and the transcendent God who is the object of faith.

Now, we have seen that if we understand man's empirical existence in terms of consciousness rather than in terms of the cognitive activity of a sub-empirical substance, truth can be understood as an existential relation of self to being which must by definition develop in order to realize itself—and not as a relation of conformity to an objective thing which must by definition be stable in order to be at all. This understanding of truth would *begin* to suggest that there can be true evolution in the dogmas of the Christian faith: it would at least obviate the objection that a true dogmatic evolution would imply either unfaithfulness to the truth of the original doctrine or the affirmation of some falsity in the same. However, the problem runs deeper. A theory of development must account not only for the possibility of *ontogenetic* but also *phylogenetic* development.

The development of the truth of the faith of the individual believer might be admitted, yet accounted for by the natural inability of man to become conscious all at once of the full extent of the revealed doctrine. The apostles themselves might be pointed out as examples of a gradual realization of a doctrine which, however, had been revealed to them long before their last communication with Jesus. This would be but a modification of the explicitation theory already discussed, permitting an increase in the articles of faith only by reason of the weakness of the human mind to take in immediately all that, in principle, it might well have absorbed from the beginning. The corollary of this would be that once revelation were fully disclosed to man for the first time—as it was to the Church before the death of the last apostle—the development of any individual's understanding of the doctrines of faith would be in effect but a catching up with the apostolic doctrine—though for historical reasons the Church's later explicitation of what the apostles implicitly believed takes the form of an increase in the articles of faith. But the dogmas of the faith of the Church as a whole would remain essentially and substantially the same. The increase in the articles of faith would be a remedy for the imperfection of individuals (and of history) rather than a positive perfection of the Church as a whole. The development of dogma would be neither normal nor desirable in itself. The problem is, therefore, whether we can account for the development of the Christian dogma *of the Church* in such a way that we can affirm simultaneously (a) the original truth of Christian doctrine, (b) the qualitative increase in the truth of Christian doctrine at later historical stages, (c) the irreducibility of a later stage of development to an earlier one, and, nevertheless, (d) that "revelation, constituting the object of the Catholic faith, was completed with the apostles."[15]

The answer depends in part on how strictly we understand the last proposition. If it is taken in the strict sense (most likely intended by the authors of *Lamentabili*), the task is impossible. For the proposition would amount to saying that the development of dogma is impossible. But if we assume that development is a fact, then this proposition should be upheld only in a very wide sense. It would be understood to mean not that revelation was an event that, once having occurred in the past, in due time ceased altogether to be, and is related to the present only by way of having set inalterable precedents. The proposition would not deny that revelation is a living, continuous and ever present historical fact, namely, the fact that the self-same God reveals himself unwaveringly, unhesitatingly, consistently and unreservedly throughout history, and not merely at one given moment

[15] *Lamentabili Sane,* Proposition 21 (DS 3421).

of time. In other words, the alternative to the strict understanding of this proposition is not that there have been further additional revelations which have proposed new objects of faith, but rather that the same original self-revelation endures and is continuously offered to man throughout history. It means, conversely, that revelation has not ended and indeed never shall as long as God continues to deal personally with man and be present to human history. For we should not suppose that the fullness of God's self-revelation in Jesus means that God's self-revelation ceased at a certain point in time, after which we no longer enjoy the revealing presence of God, but only the *record* of the revelation completed in the past.

If we are not held to a more restricted understanding of the "closing" of revelation, then the task may not be impossible. To proceed, we should note that so far we have dealt with consciousness under somewhat abstract conditions. The philosophical tradition which conceives man's psychic life as cognition (plus consequent volition) necessarily supposes that knowledge, being a potentiality of man's nature, actually occurs in real life when an individual mind somehow proceeds to posit individual acts of knowledge. We have, likewise, so far supposed that consciousness is a phenomenon which occurs in single, individual instances and in the form of private events. We have assumed that selves emerge with the same degree of individuality with which mushrooms appear in a lawn once certain botanical preconditions have been satisfied. In point of fact this is not so. Even in the case of knowledge (rather than consciousness) a sufficient reason for the actualization of the potency must be supposed. Thus, Aristotle supposed a natural inclination of human nature, "all men by nature desire to know."[16] If, on the other hand, we do not need the initial fillip of an *a priori* "natural inclination" to set *con-*

[16] *Metaphysics,* I, 1, (980 a 21).

sciousness in motion, the reason is not that unlike knowledge consciousness is by nature an ontological rather than a psychological process (for if it were an *individual* ontological process it would still require it); the reason is that it is a *socio-historical* process. In other words, consciousness does not begin within a man's *biography*. It emerges in the *social history* of man. It is part of the process of biological evolution. If we leave aside the evidence of anthropology, palaeontology, biology and genetic psychology, the philosophical evidence for this is a twofold empirical observation. All human consciousness is cast in concepts, and, conversely, conceptualization is the elementary cultural process by which animal knowledge becomes elaborated into the psychic life which is proper to man.

The cultural nature of conceptual knowledge has not been recognized by philosophy until fairly recent times. The fact that human experience took a conceptual form was explained on the assumption of a twofold dichotomy of man's psychic life. In the first place, it was dichotomized into *sensation* and *intellection*. The former, which man shared with animals, accounted for immediate experience as such. The second, accordingly, was removed from immediate experience: this left open the way for the theory that concepts were the result of an abstraction of the potentially intelligible from the actually sensible. The communicability of concepts was, therefore, interpreted as a consequence of two facts: (a) the possibility that several minds might abstract the same intelligible object; (b) the possibility of conventional agreement on signs to represent such abstractions. Hence, man's psychic life was dichotomized in a second way, namely, into *thought* and *language*.

The superficial plausibility of this second dichotomy was enhanced by the fact that, indeed, one could think without talking *out loud.* But the dichotomy went, beyond this, to suppose that the *behavioral* complex we call *language* should be understood strictly *logically,* that is, as a set of pointers or signs which indicated their corresponding concepts, but which, unlike concepts, were conventionally determined. The analysis of linguistic *behavior,* however, has shown that this interpretation does not do justice to the facts. Genetic, anthropological and philological research also indicates otherwise. Even the absurdity of this supposition has now become noticeable: by what means of communication, if not some sort of language, could men communicate in order to arrive at language conventions?[17] Likewise, the understanding of human experience as conscious forbids a real distinction between sensation and intellection.[18] In place of this dichotomy we are left with an empirically verifiable distinction between human *experience* and human *conceptualization,* that is, a distinction between the immediate reality of our "mental" life insofar as it is individually and personally our own, and the reality of our "mental" life insofar as it is represented and communicable (whether to ourselves or to others) in and through concepts.

We may understand better the empirical distinction, yet ontological unity, between our immediate experience (which is our personal consciousness) and our public, socio-historical conscious experience, cast in the concepts by which we represent our personal consciousness both to ourselves and to others, if we note that concepts give a typical human form to human experience. The *human* form of human experience is a *social* form. Con-

[17] Ludwig Wittgenstein, *Philosophical Investigations,* (Oxford, 1953), I, 25 & 338 *et passim.*

[18] It forbids a distinction between *human* sensation and *human* understanding. This does not take away the distinction between animal knowledge, which is sensation, and human sensation, which is intellectual.

ceptualization consists in giving a social form to animal, physiological psychism. Conversely, conceptualization, symbolization or linguification (the last to be physiologically distinguished from verbalization) is the fashioning of human experience as such, out of the sensory physiology of animals, by casting it in a cultural form. Human knowledge or "intellection," (that is, conceptual, linguistic experience), appears at a certain moment of biological evolution, namely, when the individually circumscribed psychic life of animals is elevated to the level of a common psychic life among many selves. It is, therefore, a socio-historical process that marks the emergence of strictly *human* experience. Thus, wherever specifically human experience exists, there we find consciousness. And wherever we find consciousness, we find it under the concrete cultural form of given concepts.

This means: consciousness is not an essentially and originally private event afterwards communicated (through signs) to other human beings. Its essential privacy and its originally personal nature are strictly relative to its essentially public and originally social and historical nature. The only truth to the idea that human experience is originally private is that before he became human man was an animal. But now that he is a social animal—that is, now that he is not an animal at all—his *human* experience is essentially and originally a social event. Conceptualization is the socio-historical process by which consciousness, and man as such, evolve.

But if human experience and consciousness are constant concomitants, can there be a legitimate, *empirically grounded* distinction between them? We have long assumed that there was not. Two reasons bolstered this assumption. The first was the very concomitance of experience and consciousness. In other words, we were not aware of man's evolutionary nature and history or, indeed, of the nature of evolution. More precisely, we were unaware (a) that man has evolved from the animal, and (b) that as he has evolved from the animal he has altogether ceased to be an animal. Though we had long suspected both these propositions and had, on occasion, held either one or the other, not until recently were we in a position to hold both integrally and simultaneously. This is why the history of philosophical anthropology has been, in a sense, the history of our attempt to understand how man both *is* and *is not* an animal. But the only alternatives we had devised until the twentieth century were all equally unsatisfactory: (a) that man was nothing but an animal, (b) that man was not and had never been an animal, (c) that man was partly an animal and partly not. The possibility open to us today is that of understanding the relation of man to the animal as a *historical* one. Man is the being that *was* an animal, though he is not *now* an animal any more. But this is not to say that he is even now unrelated to the animal. Man's *present* history is an *ex-animal* one. Well, then, experience and consciousness are related likewise.

The second reason why we had long misunderstood the relations of experience and consciousness is that they were obscured by the brilliance of our theories of knowledge. The traditional distinction between (human) sensation and understanding seemed to make the concomitance of consciousness and experience a mere consequence of the peculiarly human "spirituality" of knowledge. Thus, the communicability of conceptual knowledge through some system of conventional signs (a property that supposedly followed immediately upon the universality of concepts, and ultimately upon the spirituality of human knowledge), assumed that experience precisely as conceptual was an "inner," individual and private phenomenon which nonetheless was apt

mate teaching authority for the benefit of the faith of the Church as a whole. The "privilege" of infallibility is thus essentially related to the *eschatological* nature of the Church as a *believing community*—yet it is these very three essential aspects of infallibility, its relativity to the historicity of Christianity, to the fidelity of the Church and to the social dimension of Christian history, that are not infrequently subordinated to the *certainty, safety* and *security* that it supposedly provides. Moreover, what is a privilege for the Church as a whole might perhaps be conceived as a function, a duty and a service to be provided by the teaching authority. I mean, a service for the Christian faith; the magisterium's infallibility is not in the service of the truth of eternally valid propositions; it exists for the sake of the believing Church. Infallibility, thus, can hardly mean that the teaching of the magisterium is always as adequate as it could be—it only means that it is not less adequate than it absolutely must be if the Christian faith is to survive. It does not mean that the teaching authority can in no way fail to serve and respond to the needs of the Church, or that it cannot fall short of what at any given time the Church should have grown to believe. In brief, infallibility is a *minimal* requirement of dogma. It might be unwise to assume that it is the most that should be expected of the magisterium of the Church.[6]

[6] I have already suggested that orthodoxy, likewise, is the absolutely *minimal* requirement of Christian teaching, authoritative or otherwise: the adequacy, effectiveness, appositeness and usefulness of teaching scarcely depend on it alone. But it is ironic that the Catholic Church as a whole is beginning to experience this consciously for the first time in the very teaching of "infallibility" by Vatican I. While it cannot be denied that the Council's conceptualization of the matter in terms of "infallibility" retained the traditional Christian faith in its own eschatological relation to God's Word, nevertheless there is some reason to think that it is inadequate to the maintenance and development needs of Christian belief in modern times—and indeed that it may have been so from the outset.

to be *translated* into language, that is, into "external," social and public phenomena. The facts that somehow no human being had ever had human experience except of a cultural form, and that no man ever thought except in a language which was not-private and which he had not invented himself, but which on the contrary was public, socially shared and which had emerged within human history[19]—these facts were interpreted as mere coincidences which in no way precluded the possibility that a human being might one day come into being and, in the absence of all social and historical relations, so exist and experience that without any linguistic skills he could, if given enough time, make up his own conceptual lexicon entirely within his head and without any overt linguistic behavior. (Indeed, had not the first man—or at least the first men—evidently proceeded to invent language after he, or they, were *already* human?) And if these coincidences did not appear suspicious, it was because they were neatly and perfectly balanced by this other coincidence, namely, the coincidence of each and every concept, of each and every "inner" phenomenon, of each and every "mental word," with some corresponding "outer" or public word.

With the substitution of consciousness for assimilative knowledge the distinction between language and thought disappears.[20] But this automatically raises another question: whether experi-

[19] Wittgenstein, I, 32.

[20] The distinction between thought expressed to another consciousness, or voiced language, and thought expressed only to oneself, that is, mute or voiceless language, must obviously remain. But "private" thought is, though voiceless, language, and is as much a culturally and historically conditioned phenomenon as voiced language. Moreover, genetic psychology has shown that "private" thought is posterior to voiced language. The child does not first learn to think and afterwards learns to talk. He first learns to talk, that is, think out loud, and afterwards learns to inhibit the voicing of his thought.

ence and consciousness must not be identified. Is not human experience *as such* the same as consciousness, that is, conceptualized experience?

As a logician would say, this is a complex question; it does not admit of an unqualified answer. If there is no distinction between language and thought, there can be no distinction between "inner" experience and "outer" expression. Therefore, neither experience nor consciousness are private, that is, "inner," phenomena; both are public and social events even if they are the events *of* private persons and *of* individual selves. The question, therefore, really means: Is there a real distinction between individual human beings and human society? The answer is only partially that individuals are really distinct from society and culture. The other integral parts are that (a) individuals are, precisely as human, of a social nature, and (b) human society is composed exclusively of human individuals and has no reality apart from such individuals. Human experience, likewise, is conceptualized precisely insofar as it is human. It is the conceptualization of experience which makes man conscious and human. Thus conceptualization and consciousness are social phenomena. To put it conversely, the thinking of individual selves is not an individual, but a social and cultural phenomenon. This does not mean that societies and cultures think apart from the thinking of individuals. But neither does it mean that societies and cultures do not think at all. It means that they *do* think, but that they think *only* in and through the thinking of individuals. Similarly, it does not mean that individuals do not think, nor that individuals think apart from the society and culture in which they exist. It means that individuals *do* think, but that they think *only* in a society and through a cultural means, namely, concepts.

Let us say, then, that concepts are the *cultural form* of human experience. A cultural form is not imposed upon a pre-existing human experience. Human experience *as such* requires conceptualization and, therefore, a cultural form. Psychic life reaches the level of specifically human experience only as it receives (in conceptualization) a cultural form. Thus, no given cultural form (or conceptualization) is specifically required by human experience. And yet, every human experience requires, in order to exist, some concrete cultural conceptual form or another.

The sign of this is that although language is "natural" to man—not indeed that it is simply fitting and proper to his nature, but that he needs it in order to be human—no given language is the natural language of man. There are, no doubt, more or less perfect languages. There are, after all, more or less perfect societies.[21] But all linguistic behavior is human and all human behavior is linguistic. It follows from this that concepts and conceptual systems (languages, cultural forms) are *translatable,* but not *equivalent*. They truly differ from each other (as any person fluent in several tongues or thor-

[21] It might be objected that the perfection of societies does not necessarily go together with the development of language. On the contrary, it might be suggested that they do. But we should not restrict our concept of language to its most elementary and everyday forms. For instance, political organization is a system of linguistic behavior. And science is really scientific thinking, scientific language. For "talking" is the human way to relate human existence to reality (including that of other human beings). The scientist is a man who can talk scientifically about the world, that is, a man placed in a certain existential situation which relates him scientifically to the world. This is why science confers power on man. It is not because "the secrets of nature" having been wrested from her, nature can be blackmailed at will. It is, on the contrary, because science helps man establish friendly relations with nature. We can manage the world (or ourselves) physically only to the degree that we manage it (or ourselves) conceptually.

oughly familiar with several cultures well realizes). At the same time, one and the same human being can make a transition from one concept to its counterpart in another culture, or from one conceptual system to another. The point is that "sentences in different languages become synonymous only when they are translations of one another; they are not synonymous before they are translations."[22] To be sure, at a certain superficial level of experience one can *merely* translate, encipher and encode. But to master a foreign language is to acquire a new conceptual system: it is not simply to learn new verbal signs for the same concepts. It is, therefore, a genuine expansion of experience, in the sense that the later stage of experience grows out of the earlier but is not reducible to it. Moreover, within each culture we find a constant expansion and development, a constant re-interpretation and re-casting of experience, a constant re-thinking and re-conceptualization of the culture itself. In short, the development of human consciousness means the development of concepts and conceptual systems. Man develops culturally in order to exist.

I must digress briefly to indicate why, in the light of the linguistic nature of conceptual experience, the theory of dogmatic development already rejected above (that development is an explicitation of the implicit), is not substantially improved by adding that the explicitation of dogma translates the self-same traditional truths into a new, more communicative "language"—whether the new "language" (that is, the new verbal system or tongue) be more communicative because the communicands have forgotten the original tongue with the passage of time, or because the newer tongue is intrinsically more sophisticated or otherwise

[22] Richard Hinners, *Ideology and Analysis: a rehabilitation of metaphysical ontology,* (New York, 1966), p. 152.

more adequate to express the same truth (indeed, the same concepts) already expressed in the original tongue.

This theory of development has had a certain apologetic value. It has tended to justify change in the eyes of those who recognized its inevitability but who were fearful of it, providing as it does the comfortable suggestion that nothing of any real importance has changes when only language has changed. But it is doubtful that it could actually account for the past history of development of Christian dogma. It is more doubtful still that a program of consciously undertaken dogmatic development to serve the needs of the present and the future of Christianity could be satisfactorily pursued within the limitations of this theory.

Of course, even a mere *translation* of Christian doctrine into a tongue intelligible to modern man would indeed be a boon—this is but an indication that Christianity's conscious decision, especially since the end of the eighteenth century, to avoid developing dogma so far as possible, not only implied a theoretically mistaken notion of the relation of dogma to culture, but was also practically disadvantageous: the normal development of man's general experience was bound eventually to alienate contemporary experience from the meaning of an un-developing Christian doctrine. Thus, the fact that even a change of tongue alone (to the extent that it is possible to do this alone), would be beneficial is a measure of the depth of our needs. The point, however, is that a change of tongue brings in tow consequences that go beyond "mere words." More precisely: to the degree that Christianity *merely* changed its language (and, as I have said, this is possible at certain levels of experience, as when a message is encoded), the needs of the Church would not be well served, since what is required is the re-conceptualization of Christian dogma. On the other hand, even a change in mere language would begin to serve that need—because in point of fact it would be impossible to hold it down to a *mere* change in language. It would be but the prelude to the process known to sociologists as *acculturation*.[23] (Those "conservatives" in the Church who opposed the introduction of the vernacular into the liturgy were unquestionably right to suspect that if the Church gave up Latin it could not retain its long-traditional cultural form—and would therefore ultimately undergo more than "accidental" change.)

In sum: to master the "language" of contemporary experience is in reality to think in contemporary concepts—and to think in new concepts is to develop one's original experience. But the mere *translation* of the same doctrine into new "words" would hardly solve the problem of the *development* of dogma. A theory that would solve it would have to account for the development of the very *concepts* which express and constitute the Christian doctrine and, at the same time, for the faithful continuity of the truth of that doctrine.

If truth is the mind's conforming intentional reflection of reality through the mediation of mental concepts, faithful continuity of the truth through developing concepts is a contradiction in terms: any change in conceptual knowledge would imply a change in the mind's conformity to reality. Therefore, a more adequate conformity would imply a previous falsity. Conversely, the truth of earlier concepts would preclude any substantial improvement in their adequation (except, as previously noted, by explicitation, or in the outward verbal expression of the same concept). However, if concepts are not the medium whereby the mind relates itself to reality in a conformity-relation of truth, but

[23] Cf. Arnold Toynbee, "The psychology of encounters," in *The World and the West,* (New York, 1963), pp. 277–288.

the cultural form in which human experience is cast, the relation to reality which we call truth is, as the property of human conscious experience, not tied down to the substantial stability of concepts. Since human experience requires conceptualization for the sake of its own perfection (that is, for the sake of the emergence of this specifically human character of consciousness), and nevertheless requires by its nature as experience no determinate conceptualization, it follows that truth is achieved *in* conceptualization, but not *by means of* any given determinate concept. Unless a concept is the means whereby an intelligible reality is assimilated, truth is achieved when experience becomes human, that is, conscious, and, therefore, conceptualized. If so, truth does not depend upon the conformity of experience to being by means of some determinate concept which uniquely represents the envisaged being. Rather, it would depend upon the realization (that is, the actual coming-into-being), of human experience precisely as human (that is, of consciousness), as consciousness differentiates itself from the world (that is, relates itself to itself and to an-other).

Although truth is not the adequation of the *intellect* to *being* (insofar as understanding consists in the assimilation of being by the formal mediation of concepts), truth might nevertheless be called an adequation of *man* to *reality,* in the sense that it is *man's self-achievement* within the requirements of *a given situation.* We can call it an adequation provided we keep in mind that since man as such has the reality of being, adequation is not the human substance's transition from non-being to being in the accidental order of cognition. In this context *adequation* would not connote *conformity, correspondence, likeness* or *similarity.* It would connote *adjustment, usefulness, expediency, proficiency, sufficiency* and *adaptation.* The establishment of man's relation

of truth to reality can only be an intensification of the reality that man *already* has. It follows from this that the nature of truth does not merely permit truth to develop, but indeed requires that it do so. For truth itself consists in a certain intensive development of man's original relation to reality given by the fact that, being a reality, he participates in being. The truth of human experience is the result of consciousness' incessantly tending towards being—a tendency which, far from satisfied by the achievement of its goal, is further intensified by whatever success it may meet. Hence, the only valid "criterion" of truth is that it create the possibility of more truth. And the most reliable sign that we are coming to the truth is that we are dissatisfied with it. The presence of being to itself which takes place in consciousness is not given once for all. It is a presence that can only be described as a process of emergence, constant growth and self-creation. Unless forcibly self-restrained (which cannot be done indefinitely or without undesirable consequences), consciousness automatically leads to its own heightening. Therefore, the more conscious we become, the more conscious we can become. The more we know, the more we can know. On this basis it may be possible to suggest the outline of a theory of the mechanism of dogmatic development in which the very preservation of the original truth of Christianity would not merely permit, but actually require, the ceaseless re-conceptualization of Christian belief. Such a theory would rest on the distinction between the *experience* and the *conceptualization* of faith. The meaning of this distinction should be clear from what precedes.

In the Scholastic tradition there is a distinction between, on the one hand, the habit and the act of faith, and the articles of faith, on the other. This might seem at first to correspond to the distinction between the experience of faith and its conceptualization. But this would be incorrect. In Scholasticism the articles of faith are the formal signs *quo,* by means of which the object *quod,* revelation, is *attained* in the act of faith. In the distinction suggested here, the concepts in which the faith is articulated are rather the formal means by which the human experience of faith (in which man is related to that-which-is-revealed by a relation of faith) comes into being precisely as human, that is, as conscious. For, evidently, there is no infra-human religious experience.[24] If all religious experience attains to some level of consciousness, the conceptualization by which religious experience comes into being as consciousness is not superadded to some prior assimilation of an object of revelation by the intellect. The conceptualization of faith is a process by which we render ourselves *present* to that-in-which-we-believe. This does not mean that concepts perform the function of mediating the mind's assimilation of reality: the concepts which articulate and express the Christian faith do not render us present to that-in-which-we-believe by virtue of their alleged representational value. They are not "similitudes" of their object. (In what way, other than as required to validate a theory of knowledge, could the concepts *God* or *man* be said to be "like" God or man?) Like all other concepts, the concepts of Christian belief are not true because of their effectiveness in representing objects. They are true because of their effectiveness in relating (by a relation of truth) man's reality to the reality of that-in-which-he-believes. And this effectiveness in producing the truth of belief is the same as their effectiveness, as a form of experience, in producing the emergence of conscious experience. This refers both to their effectiveness

[24] An animal exists in the physical presence of God in the same way as man does, yet evidently cannot have even a "natural" religious experience. The reason is that it cannot have conceptual experience at all.

in the *emergence* of current consciousness, and their effectiveness in facilitating the further *intensification* of consciousness.

Truth, therefore, is attributable to Christian belief by reason of the latter's character as religious experience—an experience, to be sure, which would not be human or, therefore, religious unless it were cast in the form of specific concepts. This means, as I have suggested, that the concepts in which Christian belief are cast are true, not in virtue of their representative adequacy, but in virtue of their efficacious adequacy as generative forms of the truth of religious experience. A concept is true if it causes (that is, permits the coming-into-being of) a true human experience as such (that is, as conscious). Rather—since every concept, as even the traditional epistemologies recognize, must be in some way true, for it permits the establishment of some relation to reality in human consciousness—it would be better to say that the concept is true *to the degree* that by its elevation of experience to consciousness it permits the truth of human experience to come into being.

There should be no difficulty in admitting that Christian belief is a religious experience—the context of this proposition should make it clear that religious experience does not consist in any sort of mystical intuition.[25] Religious experience is, as experience, different from no other experience—it is a conscious awareness of the same epistemological order as ordinary "knowledge." Its difference from ordinary knowledge has to do with that *of which* it is an experience, namely, a transcendent reality first adumbrated negatively in the empirical apprehension of the contingency of our own being. This difference, in turn, accounts for two further properties. First, unlike ordinary knowledge, faith is the conscious experience of something *inevident,*

[25] I do not, on the other hand, deny that mystical intuitions are possible, however extraordinary they may be.

something which unlike *this desk* and *this chair* is not seen to be *there,* even if it enters into the fabric of our personal relations to reality with at least as much force, relevance and moment as things which are seen to be *there*. Second, unlike knowledge, faith must be said, as in the traditional Christian expression, to be due to God's initiative. We can, in principle, get away from anything we do not want to experience or, conversely, become present to anything we may want to experience. But belief or disbelief in God is the kind of experience that we can neither procure at will nor get away from. (Nevertheless, insofar as faith is man's *free response* to that initiative, it continues to share in the nature of all human experience.)

Consequently, the Christian faith is never found in the state of a "pure" religious experience—any more than it can be found in the assent of an act of judgment in relation to that which is "presented" by a concept. In reality the Christian experience of faith can be found only as conceptualized and, therefore, under one cultural form or another. It follows that the Christian tradition's continuity in truth does not essentially reside in the absoluteness of the cultural form that it takes at any given time—not even in that of its earliest or original cultural form—nor therefore in that of the concepts in which it is cast, (although such continuity in truth requires the continuity of God's self-communication to man, and the continuity of man's correlative religious experience in response to God's initiative).[26] This is not,

[26] The theory of doctrinal development sketched here bears some real, but many superficial resemblances to the so-called Modernist theory, perhaps most obviously at this point. Therefore, I should point out certain essential differences between the two.

The Modernist theory of development (at least as defined and condemned by *Pascendi* [DS 3475 ff.], which is the only one that matters for present purposes), is in summary as follows. Since God does not reveal propositions or formulae about himself, he does not truly reveal himself except insofar as he implants in man an immanent religious sense or

therefore, the continuity of sameness, or the continuity of that which remains (substantially) unchanged in the midst of (accidental) change. Truth cannot remain *the same.* It would make as little sense to say that existence remains *the same,* that one

---

consciousness, and an impulse towards the divine. Christianity is a revealed religion only insofar as it is the evolutionary development of man's religious experience or consciousness [for the Modernists did not distinguish between the two]. That is, Christianity is the development of the original principles immanent in human nature. Therefore, the Judaeo-Christian "revelation" is not essentially different from any other; it is much like that of any natural religion (except in that, having followed its own evolutionary line, it differs in specific content, in a great many dogmas, from other religions). Thus, the conceptualization of religious consciousness, religious sentiment or religious experience has no other purpose than to furnish the believer with a means of giving to himself an account of his faith. Dogmas, therefore, are symbols which stand between the believer and his faith. They must evolve because they are in essence, and precisely as dogmatic symbols, inadequate. They were originally inadequate and shall always remain so. All this assumes, of course, that revelation was in no sense completed with the close of the apostolic age. Revelation is rather a perpetual unfolding of the religious sense immanent in man's nature.

A theory of development in accordance with the views expressed here would contest each and every one of these propositions. It would instead propose that although God does not reveal propositions or formulae or concepts about himself, he truly reveals himself. He does this not through a principle immanent in human nature. He does it personally, by his own agency, through his personal presence to human history, in which he freely chooses to appear and take part. Although we cannot deny to God the possibility of acting in all human history and to reveal himself in other ways, his revelation to man in the Judaeo-Christian tradition is unique and extraordinary: the Christian religion and the Catholic Church are, in this extraordinary and unique sense, the true religion and the true Church to which all men are called. The conceptualization of religious experience of faith does not come between man and the object of faith: on the contrary, it enables the experience of faith to exist. Dogmatic formulae and concepts, therefore, do not mediate between faith and its object: they express faith in its object, God. Therefore, they evolve not because they are always and from the beginning necessarily inadequate, but because as man develops they become inadequate if they fail to evolve. They must, therefore, in a sense necessarily develop, since man himself must develop in order to exist. And revelation was completed with the close of the apostolic age at least in the sense that, the Redemption having been accomplished as a

moment of consciousness is *the same* as another, or that life is *the same* thing over and over again. Nor is the continuity of truth a mere contiguity among truths, the merely phenomenal continuity of unbroken passage from the self-same to the different. It is rather a *faithful* continuity, that is, a continuity like

---

concrete and discrete historical event, mankind ceased to exist in the preparatory period of *Heilsgeschichte* and henceforth would exist in the final historical age of *man* in his relations with God, that is, in the "new and eternal testament." But this does not mean that within the age of the Incarnation there can be no further development of mankind's faith-response to God's continuous self-revelation nor, therefore, in the dogmas that conceptualize and formulate that belief. (Nor, incidentally, does it mean that there could not be a further stage of divine-human relations beyond the "new and eternal testament" of *man's* last historical age if, at the "end of the world," man should evolve altogether beyond humanity.) On the contrary, as man, by his natural powers, develops and becomes more perfectly aware of himself and the world, it is necessary that the conceptualization of his religious faith develop correspondingly in order to preserve if not also perfect his original faith in the self-same self-revealing God.

The fundamental mistake of the Modernists consisted in attempting to reinterpret the traditional doctrines of the development of dogma and of the nature of revelation in line with the contemporary awareness of human evolution and historicity, but on the continued assumption of the traditional theory of knowledge, in which a subject enters into union with an object to overcome an original isolation between the two. If so, the only alternative to the traditional idea that God's revelation was essentially and uniquely cast in the original concepts employed by Scripture, is the idea that it was cast in an immanent religious sentiment and inclination as part of the original constitution of human nature. In the theory of knowledge suggested here human knowledge is not the bridging of an original isolation but, on the contrary, the self-differentiation of consciousness in and through its objectification (of the world and of itself); and conceptualization is the socio-historical mechanism through which the self-differentiation of consciousness can take place. Concepts are not the *subjective* expression of an *objective* reality (nor, therefore, a means whereby we become reflectively conscious of a self which already existed prior to reflection), Concepts are the self-expression of consciousness and, therefore, the means by which we objectify (the world and the self), and the means whereby we self-communicate with another self (*including God*), that is, the means by which we objectify ourselves for another self, and by which we objectify ourselves for ourselves.

that of human existence itself, which embodies and brings up to the present the progress of its career and the perfection of its original inspiration. It is a continuity in which every moment is *radically new,* not as if the present moment came out of nowhere and were destined to pass into oblivion, but because it emerges from and yet brings with it its past, and because as it does so it offers the assurance that it will yet bring about the radically new future.

In this connection Karl Rahner has developed an analogy so apt that I quote it at length:

> The lover knows of his love: this knowledge of himself forms an essential element in the very love itself. The knowledge is infinitely richer, simpler and denser than any body of propositions about the love could be. Yet this knowledge never lacks a certain measure of reflexive articulateness: the lover confesses his love at least to himself, 'states' at least to himself something about his love. And so it is not a matter of indifference to the love itself whether or not the lover continues to reflect upon it; this self-reflexion is not the subsequent description of a reality which remains in no way altered by the description. In this progressive self-achievement, in which love comprehends itself more and more, in which it goes on to state something "about" itself and comprehends its own nature more clearly, the love itself becomes ordered; it has an increasing understanding of what must properly be the foundation of its own activity, mirrors its own nature with increasing clarity, approaches as its goal, with an increasingly clear awareness, what it always has been.[27]

But I would enter a demurrer against taking the illustrative value of this analogy to depend upon the specifically affective mode of consciousness with which it deals, namely, love. The point of Rahner's analogy, as I interpret it, is that consciousness ("The lover knows of his love") alters itself ("this self-reflexion is not the subsequent description of a reality which remains in no way altered by the description"), that is, it develops by reason

[27] Karl Rahner, *Theological Investigations,* vol. 1, (Baltimore and London, 1961), p. 64.

of man's self-communication, or through the presence of man's psychic life to itself. Hence, the intensification of its coming-into-being has this (apparently) paradoxical quality: that it perpetually "approaches . . . what it always has been." (Rahner, however, appears to me to neglect the socio-historical dimension of consciousness and, hence, that of dogmatic development.)

The Christian faith, thus, appears able to develop not only as a subjective and individual disposition. Its *truth* can also develop. Christian dogmas can undergo true development; they can, and in the normal course of events ought to, transform themselves culturally as their concepts undergo cultural evolution. This process can be properly called a *transformation,* because it is precisely the form that changes. It can be properly called an *evolution,* because the emergent form cannot be reduced to the act of the potentiality of the original form. And since the conceptual form of the experience of faith does not determine what is revealed, it also follows that the cultural transformation of the Christian faith and the development of its truth do not imply either the discovery of a new, different truth which it did not previously possess, or the betrayal of the truth that it previously possessed. What it *does* imply, however, is that

> truth is no longer the *adaequatio rei et intellectus* . . . But truth remains, and this truth that remains is living and active. It is the *adaequatio mentis et vitae.*[28]

The development of dogma can be understood as the historical transformation and evolution of the conceptualization of the Christian faith. This is possible because the Christian faith is not wedded to any given cultural form, any more than it is to be found as a pure essence, devoid of a concrete cultural form. As it can endure through history and transcend cultures, it can

[28] Maurice Blondel, *Carnets Intimes,* (Paris, 1961), p. 86.

transcend concepts. Therefore, the traditional Christian faith can be cast not only in the traditional concepts but also in the novel, emergent concepts that an evolving human experience creates.

The theory of development sketched here attempts to account not only for the possible future development of dogma, although its most immediate practical usefulness, if valid, would be to render possible a consciously undertaken programme of doctrinal development. It should also facilitate our understanding of the kind of development which we can retrospectively detect in the history of doctrine. For if we approach the historical facts without the presupposition that the "essence" of Christianity remained "substantially" the same between, say, apostolic times and the middle ages, it is difficult to avoid the conclusion that the typical religious experience of mediaeval man was strikingly different in form from that of primitive Jewish and hellenistic Christianity. If a first- or second-century oriental Christian had been suddenly transported through time and space to thirteenth-century Europe, it is quite possible he would have found it difficult to believe that the Catholic Church had survived, its original faith intact. Insofar as we can historically reconstruct, for any two such periods, what Christian belief must have felt like, we must speak of a real *transformation* of the Christian consciousness as it realized itself culturally and historically.

The same theory of development enables us to understand how the contemporary problems of Christianity derive from a peculiarity of the specific historical development it has undergone. The concept which even today defines Christianity's principal operative form is that of a Christian faith constituted by a dogmatic substantial essence, immutable and alone necessary, brought into existence by man's act of faith co-operating with the efficiency of divine grace, and distinguishable from its contingent, accidental cultural manifestations. This self-concept, which has increasingly demanded an artificial and unnatural fixity of Christianity, is explainable by a simple cause: it is the self-understanding to which Christianity was bound to arrive once it adopted along with its post-Judaic, hellenic cultural form, the basic metaphysical notions of hellenic thought. In the same way, if we consider the history of the second millennium of Christianity we are likely to conclude that the progressive alienation between the Christian faith and the secular, real-life experience of mankind, can be principally accounted for by the artificial maintenance of a cultural form of Christianity, namely, the hellenic, which was gradually (but with accelerating rapidity over the last century and a half), outstripped by a historical development of human consciousness characterized above all by its progressive de-hellenization.

This suggests a final reflexion. Is there any intrinsic need, due in fidelity to the Christian faith, to believe that the basic metaphysical notions of the Greek philosophical tradition are true? Granted that they may well be true, must Christians *believe* they are true on the grounds that they are indispensable for upholding the current self-understanding of the Christian faith? Or does it not seem more reasonable to suppose that their adoption and use by the Christian faith must be conditioned by their proven usefulness, that is, by their independent truth? If a Christian believer first adopts Greek metaphysics, he must in good logic understand Christianity as consisting of an immutable dogmatic essence. But if he does not, can there be anything in the revealed doctrine of Christianity to require him to understand Christianity in such terms? The question answers itself.

If there were, it would mean that there existed one form, the definitive form, of Christian dogma which was necessary and immutable precisely because it was unrelated to human consciousness, culture and history. The impossibility of this position has not been manifest as long as we have assumed either of these positions: that conceptual knowledge was likewise unrelated to culture, or that some given culture provided the only legitimate conceptual form of Christian religious experience. This might be put more graphically in an epigram: we can search for the essence of Christianity behind its cultural manifestations only as long as we assume either that we can become conscious of God's self-revelation without God's use of any human language (Modernism), or else that God's mother tongues are Hebrew and Greek (Scholasticism).

In opposition to this view, the theory of development sketched above would find the criterion of orthodoxy and of the faithful continuity of the Christian tradition, not in the constancy of a sub-cultural substantial reality called Christian truth, but within the very transformations of Christianity as an essentially cultural reality. In this conception, therefore, the truth of Christianity is a historical, not an eternal, one. Christianity has a contingent, factual, temporal truth, because contingency, factuality and temporality are the notes of God's historical presence and self-revelation to man.

4.

The Underdevelopment of Christian Theism

I HAVE suggested that Christian belief finds in the conscious experience of lived existence both the absence and the presence of God. If so the faith of Christian theism is not the intentional possession of a heavenly object by means of a supernaturally modified cognitive power. For faith is not, in the first place, an intentional possession of an object by means of the exercise of a cognitive faculty. Faith is an ascent to God—a metaphor that is adequate only if we do not imagine the success of the journey to consist in reaching some object placed at the summit. Its achievement is in the ascending, not in the end: at its highest point, as St. John of the Cross declared, faith finds not an object, but "nothing."[1] The "mystical" union with God, which is nothing else than the perfection of the Christian life of faith, is therefore consistently described by him in the antithetical terms

[1] "*Y en el monte nada.*" It is interesting to note that in the diagram that prefaces St. John of the Cross's *The Ascent of Mount Carmel, caritas,* which introduces the soul to the plateau of *convivium* with God in the *divinum silentium* and the *divina sapientia,* is reached by surmounting *securitas.* Diego de Astor's original diagram, mistakenly attributed in many editions to John himself, is reproduced in Crisógono de Jesús and Lucinio del SS. Sacramento, *Vida y Obras de San Juan de la Cruz,* (Madrid, 1946), p. 1273.

of *presence* and *absence*. In this respect he is in the best Christian tradition. For in this tradition belief in God is perpetually qualified by the conviction that faith, as well as knowledge, is disproportionate to the ultimate reality of God, so that no affirmation about God, not even the affirmation that he exists, can be truthfully made unless it is complemented by a negation. And insofar as this negation is itself affirmed, it must be surmounted by some type of synthetic affirmation, for example the "superlative" theology of the Pseudo-Dionysius, or the *via eminentiae* of St. Thomas.[2]

But whatever solution has been given to thc antithesis, it has always been clear that simple affirmation is incompatible with the truthfulness of Christian belief. The transcendence of God makes it necessary both to deny and to affirm: God is beyond existing and non-existing. (I do not say that we have always found it possible to abide by this paradox, or to conceive superlative affirmations that were irreducible to simple theses.) The point is that we cannot adequately believe in God unless these qualifications and this relative disbelief become integrating parts of our lived faith. For if their effective role is merely that of rhetorical devices whereby to escape the difficulties of relative theism, our faith suffers, and we are then apt to lapse into the far easier absolute theism. Conversely, an unqualified belief in God, an absolute and unconditional affirmation of God, is not what the Christian tradition calls *faith*. It is a *distortion* of faith. The Christian tradition calls it *credulity*.

Insofar as Judaeo-Christianity is in uninterrupted temporal and cultural continuity with the history of man, the divine, revealed origin of its distinctive faith should be understood as a historical event, that is, as occurring within the history of man's emergence

[2] St. Thomas, *In De divinis nominibus,* I, 2–3; *ST,* I, 12, 13.

from credulity. (Marx was perfectly right to judge that the fundamentalist understanding of the origin of the Judaeo-Christian religion could appear only ridiculous to anyone who shared the contemporary level of human self-awareness.) It follows that the most fundamental and original sense in which faith is a gratuitous gift from God, is in the sense that the nature of man, though open to the possibility of developing faith out of credulity, does not of itself necessitate such a development. Moreover, the emergence of faith, in the Christian sense of the word, does not guarantee its maintenance and perpetuation. Faith can be maintained only in the process of its constant self-realization and self-purification, that is, in the process of its constant overcoming of credulity. We have already observed that Christian theism forever seeks to surpass itself as it overcomes the inevidence of God. Well, the Christian faith seeking forever to realize itself and its truth by overcoming credulity complements that observation.

We are thus in a position to distinguish between two moments in the development of the Christian faith. The first moment is positive, and it consists in overcoming inevidence. The second is negative, and it consists in overcoming credulity. This distinction is useful. It should help us understand why the history of Christianity shows not one, but two, distinct ways in which it has failed to develop its theism as adequately as it might.

THE NORMAL UNDERDEVELOPMENT OF CHRISTIAN THEISM

There is a first inadequacy in the development of the Christian faith which is but the necessary consequence of the inevidence of God. It tells us more about faith insofar as it depends on the nature of God than it does about faith insofar as it depends on its nature as a conscious response of man to his experience of the transcendent. All that will be said here on this point is that such formulae as "God is and always shall remain a mystery" would be thoroughly misleading if, instead of being taken as *revealing* something of God himself, that he *is* of such a nature that his relations to us must be mysterious, they were taken as indicating the *un-revealing* character of revelation: that God has chosen to be mysterious out of some inexplicable caprice—or perhaps that man's fallenness has removed him from his proper home in the divine light to an earthly exile in the darkness of the world. We can, on the contrary, reasonably suppose only that if God is "verily a hidden God,"[3] the reason cannot be that God is the kind of reality that might well have chosen to appear to man evidentially (say, Garden-of-Eden fashion), but has unaccountably preferred somehow to remain hidden as he reveals himself. The reason can only be that it is proper for him in his relations to man to remain "mysterious." For the transcendence of a God who *could* be seen by living man[4] would not be enough to account for what in fact is the experience of Christian belief. Such a being could elicit only credulity. If the hiddenness of God is to make sense it must be *meaningful*. It must indeed constitute the first and most basic (at least in the sense of most primitive and initial) revelation of God about himself. If so, in the fact that the reality of God must be such as to remain hidden to living man, we find the first way in which the Christian faith must remain inadequate. And this is a *normal* inadequacy. For the disproportion between man and the ultimate basis of transcendence might be morally dissolved, but it must ontologically

[3] Isa. 45, 15.
[4] Exod. 33, 20 & 23.

remain insurmountable if God is that which we believe to fill up the openness revealed by the experience of transcendence, and which is the converse of the contingency of the totality of being. In other words, we cannot "see" God, nor can he be "seen" by man until, if ever, we "deserve" it—that is, until, if ever, God is made "visible" by our realization, indeed, our *creation* of him in us. (For *morally* speaking God is made to exist—or not to exist—by man's freely chosen existence, a consideration that should suggest to us what is, instead of law, the source of moral obligation and the true measure of moral responsibility.)

But beyond that we cannot go. We can only suppose that even after we "see" God he remains "the wholly other." For to suppose otherwise would imply that God is an *object* within the totality of being. And such a being might well fit the requirements of other religions (or, if granted sufficient perfection, supremacy and infinity, those of Greek metaphysics), but it would not be the "transcendent" God of Christian belief. For God's reality is indeed within the totality of being. He is not foreign or remote to the world or to us—after all, he is not farther away than the other side of existence—and he does not inhabit a heaven outside the cosmos, since the cosmos is his home: this, too, is integral part of the God of Christian belief. But God is not comprised within the totality of the world. In a sense, therefore, he will never be reached. No matter how much man evolves and how much his consciousness, his religious experience and his faith develop, there is no foreseeable point at which we shall no longer *tend* towards God. This, then, is the *normal* inadequacy of the Christian faith. Correspondingly, Christian theism cannot expect ever to comprehend and exhaust in its concepts the reality of God. The possibility of further development shall always remain.

Now, this normal inadequacy of man's response to God can be found in the individual. But does it also affect the historical development of Christianity as a whole? It would seem not. For even if we agree that the faith of the Church does not exhaust or comprehend the mystery of God, does not the infallibility of the magisterium of the Church provide an effective substitute, not in every way, but in the sense that the faith of the Church should not be considered normally inadequate? Does not the defined dogma of infallibility forbid the idea that the Christian faith taught by the Church should be normally inadequate and less than fully achieved?

The doctrine of the infallibility of the magisterium of the Church, particularly in respect to the infallibility of the pope, would be misunderstood if one neglected the intrinsic reference of that infallibility to the faith of the Church. What is radically infallible is that faith. That is, we believe that the faith of the Church is privileged in that it shall not suffer ultimate failure, a privilege which, of course, no individual believer ever has. We would misunderstand this privilege if we so construed it as to render impossible every inadequacy short of the failure of the faith of the Church, or of its teaching by the magisterium. All the more so if we conceive it so as to render infallible the personal faith of the pope;[5] or if we conceived it as a guarantee of the wisdom, perceptiveness, good judgment, effectiveness or prudence of the magisterium or of ecclesiastical authorities. Essentially, it can only be the assurance of the *ultimately* unfailing nature of the Christian faith in and through the establishment of a legiti-

[5] Although it cannot very well be supposed that the pope's personal faith is infallible, our most common understanding of infallibility makes it ordinarily impossible to discern an apostate, heretical or superstitious pope. This is alone enough to assure us that there must be grave inadequacies to our most common understanding of the matter.

Evidently, then, beyond the normal inadequacy there can be a further inadequacy, one which the Christian faith need not have. But before we come to it we must conclude that even the collective, infallible *faith* of the Church must exhibit a normal inadequacy which derives from the disproportion of even the Church as a whole (and not merely that of individual believers) to the hiddenness of the self-revelation of God. Because of this the faith of Christianity as a whole must develop ceaselessly and forever. Correspondingly, the Christian *doctrine* must develop, both in the collective and in individual faith of the Church, in the (authoritative and non-authoritative) teaching of the Church and in the learning of every faithful, in the thought of the Christian community and in the life of the Church. The inadequacy in question is not permanently diminished by the exercise of the teaching function of the Church, even when this magisterium appeals to the infallibility of the Christian faith. Indeed, to suppose that the unfailing character of the Christian faith, afforded in and through the establishment and exercise of the magisterium, implies the total adequacy of that teaching (as if the magisterium could be said either to know the mind of God, or to comprehend the Christian truth—at least when it teaches with explicit reference to its infallibility), would be itself an inadequacy of the Christian faith—but this time an *abnormal* one, that is, one which actually detracted from the due quality of the Christian faith.

Thus, the normal inadequacy of both the individual and the collective faith of Christianity may be compounded by an unnecessary additional inadequacy which in the extreme case may border on unfaithfulness to the faith. We have thus been brought to the second inadequacy, this time one which is due to our failure or inability to live up to the Christian faith's intrinsic need for perpetual deepening and self-realization. This sort, too, is found, first, in each Christian individual as such, being attributable to factors residing within the individual believer. But as already mentioned it may also be found in that corporate institutionalization of Christian belief which we call the Church. It is the latter that will detain our attention, since it is this to which public consideration by both Christians and non-Christians pertains. I have referred to this as an *abnormal* inadequacy, in the sense that it is the kind that Christianity cannot become reconciled to. It is also abnormal in that it should appear to the Christian as an aberration from normal expectations. But no suggestion as to the frequency or rarity with which it obtains is intended by this designation. It might be better therefore to refer to it as an *unwarranted* and *inexpedient* inadequacy. What is its nature? How has it come about? How has it manifested itself?

THE ABNORMAL UNDERDEVELOPMENT OF CHRISTIAN THEISM

Let us recall certain notions broached in the previous chapters. The Christian religious experience must always take a given cultural form, without which there can be no religious experience at all. Therefore, like every other religious faith the Christian belief in God is relative to some given *concept* of God: God cannot be believed in unless he be somehow conceived. It follows that a religion that were restricted by its nature or by its self-understanding to its own culture (a henotheism, for example) would be indissolubly married to its own concept of God. But Christianity is essentially catholic. It believes itself to be essentially related to the temporal and spatial totality of men. It is for all men and all times, for all societies and all ages, for all cultures and all stages of consciousness. Christianity, therefore, implies that no given concept of God can be the unique and necessary concept of God required by Christian belief. Thus, if Christian dogma generally is required by its nature to develop constantly in the same measure that human consciousness develops so as to maintain and realize its truth, the same requirement applies to the particular case of the concept of God. Indeed, it applies to the doctrine of God with special urgency, since belief in God is, of course, the fundamental article of the Christian faith. Consequently, the development of the concept of God is crucially important in the development of Christian dogma. Underdevelopment or inadequate development of theism is the principal form of the unwarranted and inexpedient inadequacy of the Christian faith. And if the theism of Christianity, as has been suggested above, is relative and conditional, we can appreciate the reason why the underdevelopment of Christian theism automatically implies most likely a drift in the direction of absolute theism.

Despite the primitive and constant tradition of the transcendence of God, and despite the theological attempts (through some type of "superlative" theology or *via eminentiae*) to safeguard that transcendence as theological speculation proceeds, Christian theism has nevertheless tended in some ways to become absolute. This may be why many aspects of the life of the Church today appear to teach and foster belief in a somewhat primitive God. The impression seems fairly widespread that for Christianity belief in God means most basically a sincere conviction that somewhere there exists a Supreme Being, an objective reality, a person, whose principal properties are omnipotence, omniscience and infinity. The implication seems to be that the Christian faith believes in exactly the same God as any intelligent and well-disposed non-Christian might well believe in (or *know* about if he is a skilled philosopher), and that what is peculiar to Christian belief is revealed and begins *thereafter;* for instance, the divine property of there being three persons in one and the same divine nature, the historical events of man's creation, fall and redemption, etc. It is difficult to suppose that this concept of God could be propagated without the Christian faith tending to regress towards credulity.

The full answer to the question how and why the development of Christian theism should have gradually decelerated and ultimately all but ceased, so that the mere passage of time has brought us to the unwarranted and inexpedient inadequacy of contemporary theism, would require the retelling of the whole history of Christian dogma from the apostolic age until our own day. Nevertheless, it is possible to allude briefly to what was possibly the single most important factor tending to arrest the development of dogma in general and that of the concept of God very particularly. I refer again to the conclusion of historical research that the catholicization of Christianity from St. Paul to St. Augustine necessarily meant the adoption of a hellenistic cultural form. Afterwards, although the intellectual ambitions of the early second Christian millennium were not created by hellenism, they were whetted by it and were channeled in certain directions by it. And finally, through the intervention of chance historical events, notably the rediscovery of Aristotle, the hellenization of Christianity fittingly culminated in the *Weltanschauung* of medieval Scholasticism.

However, certain stipulations must be entered immediately. The first should respond to the objection registered by Catholic scholars since the nineteenth century to the concept of Christianity's hellenization. They have always been loath to accept the results of historical research, even as it has ever more clearly indicated the hellenization of Christianity as a matter of historical fact, on the *a priori* ground that hellenization would imply a substantial corruption of Christianity—a conclusion which would be incompatible with belief in Christianity's truth. It is true that many historians of dogma, notably Harnack, have not only determined the historical fact, but have also interpreted it as a corruption of the Gospel (which corruption indeed accounted for the generation of the Church). Nevertheless, for the reasons suggested in a previous chapter, the same facts could be interpreted—perhaps more adequately indeed—without the introduction of any such suspicion. Hellenization might be properly so called—being the adoption of a hellenic cultural form—without the implication that it is the substitution of the true by a false form of Christianity. (This would in good logic also carry the implication that, despite St. Paul, the earliest and original form of Christianity, namely, the Jewish, was its only true and eternally valid form.) The hellenization of Christianity was rather the gradual transformation of an earlier cultural form into a later one, it being assumed that the truth of Christianity depended on neither form as such.

Second, a case could be made for the view that the adoption of the hellenic form was not only unavoidable but indeed a providential boon, insofar as it served admirably well the contemporary purposes of developing the Christian faith by increasing its catholicity. Hellenism, after all, *was,* though not the cultural form of the whole world as we know it today, the cultural form of the *ecumenical* world. Throughout the apostolic and patristic age it was practically, and given the extant historical conditions including the stage of human knowledge and consciousness even theoretically, impossible to distinguish between the *universalization* and the *hellenization* of Christianity. The Christian faith's becoming *catholic* meant, in effect, its becoming *hellenic*. Thus, to say that the hellenic form of Christianity is inadequate to the present moment is not in the least to say that it was inadequate in the first four centuries of Christianity. Conversely, it would be anachronistic to imagine that the form which Christianity needs and can have today could or should have been remotely approximated in another age.

Finally, it follows that although the hellenic form of Christianity has truly resulted in the contemporary unwarranted inadequacy of the Christian faith, this refers not to the *adoption* of that form in the first instance, but to the failure of Christianity to continue gradually and prudently to *develop* itself beyond that cultural form as the historical need arose. On the other hand, it must be also understood that if it is much more difficult to dehellenize Christianity than it was to hellenize it, the reason has much less to do with the will and the initiative of Christians than with an intrinsic characteristic of the hellenic form: hellenization naturally and logically tended to lend Christianity the conviction that it should not develop further or transcend its hellenic form. For hellenization introduced into Christianity the ideals of immutability, stability and impassibility as perfections that all Christians and Christianity as a whole should strive for, since these were the typical and central perfections of God himself.[7]

In Christianity's hellenization we find an explanation for the paradoxical fact that in the four centuries that began with

[7] And yet, stability was by no means the most powerful idea within the culture of Greece herself. Possibly the concept of *ananke,* natural necessity (especially in its mythological form, *moira,* fate), filled that role. But in Greek *speculation* immutability and self-identity were the central properties of divine being. Therefore, they became central to hellenized Christianity, because the idea of God was central to Christianity in the first place.

Paul's missions and ended with the Council of Chalcedon there was an incredibly rapid, deep and extensive development of the Christian faith—perhaps indeed most markedly of all in what pertained to the concept of God—which suddenly came to all but a full stop as the Dark Ages descended upon the *oikumene,* not to be lifted again, temporarily, until the Carolingian prelude to the early medieval renaissance. For the development of dogma stimulated and made possible by the hellenization of Christianity meant, from another viewpoint, its petrification. For example, the swifter the Christian faith developed towards the formulations of the Trinity and the Incarnation—the heart of the Christian doctrine of God—reached at Nicaea, Constantinople and Chalcedon, the firmer its self-implication in a partly conscious, partly unconscious, commitment to a supposedly final conceptualization of its belief in the Christian God and in the person of Jesus, its founder and Christ. The briefest examination of the matter should suggest how this occurred.

THE UNDERDEVELOPMENT OF THE DOGMAS OF THE TRINITY AND THE INCARNATION

The appeal of the apostolic and early Christian Gospel pertained to the order of *praxis,* that is, existential engagement. There was in Christianity, to begin with, no distinction between preaching and teaching, *kerygma* and *didache*. The Good News concerned the historical, existential situation of man. It had to do with the restoration of the human order and the forthcoming Kingdom of God. Therefore, it called for a certain decision, namely, the decision of faith. But this meant the resolve to exist in the light of a certain understanding of the present situation. The Christian commitment, thus, unlike adherence to, say, a national religion, naturally inclined its practitioner to speculation. An existential commitment, being the exercise of creative consciousness freely developing by self-intensification,[8] is already the first step towards the theoretical development of consciousness.[9] For to exist in the light of any concept of existence is already to have entered into a process of conceptual development—and theorizing is but a mode of conceptual elaboration. In other words: the decision to heed the proclamation and teaching of Christianity created a need to bring into consciousness and to elaborate conceptually the originally obscure and merely practical faith[10] in the person of Jesus and in the God whose Kingdom he introduced.

But it would be unhistorical to suppose that at the first moment of the development of Christian consciousness this consciousness could have created the concepts whereby to elaborate itself—it is not until our own day that such a possibility has begun to emerge. At the time, all it could possibly have done was to use the concepts of which it was *already* possessed. The intellectual effort of the early centuries was, therefore, predominantly directed to the adaptation of hellenic concepts to serve the development of dogma—that is, to the casting of Christianity in hellenic forms.

Now, the absolutely most basic Christian religious experience[11]

[8] J. P. Sartre, *Critique de la raison dialectique,* (Paris, 1960), pp. 165 ff.

[9] Hinners, pp. 32–35 *et passim.*

[10] By *practical faith* I do not mean an "ethical" faith such as that of liberal Protestantism, or an "applied" faith such as that of popular Catholic belief. I mean an *ontic* faith, as contrasted with an *ontological* faith. The origin of speculative faith in practical faith (instead of the other way about, as is commonly assumed by Catholic opinion, has been shown by Hinners, *op. cit.*

[11] Let us recall the distinction between *experience* and *concept.* The most basic *concept* of the Christian faith was that of the "good news," that is, the idea that the Redemption of man from the individual and historical condition of sin had taken place, with the consequent advent of the Kingdom of God.

—at least at the level of analysis of which we are capable today—was that of a God who transcended the monotheism of the religion of the Old Testament. The primitive monotheism of Moses,[12] which had succeeded the earlier worship of "strange gods,"[13] had developed in later Jewish times into the quasi-metaphysical monotheism of Philo Judaeus and the rabbinical literature. Likewise, the faith which in time was cast in the trinitarian dogmatic formulations was a religious experience according to which over and above the uniqueness of the being who is the source of being there was the self-communication of his reality.

This means, in the first place, (as far as our religious experience is concerned), that God communicates himself to us. More precisely: what he communicates to us is himself. Revelation is no longer experienced in the New Testament as it was most commonly in the Old, namely, as the communication of a message from God. For it was now believed that God does not send a message in place of himself. He comes in person to deliver his message and, moreover, his message is not other than himself. Conversely, the "word" that he sends is an utterance (that is, something issued or sent) only in the sense that it proceeds from him, but not in the sense that what is uttered is other than himself.[14] And if what is communicated by God to us is really himself, it follows that his self-communication to us implies the self-communication of himself to himself: there must be a real

[12] William F. Allbright, *From the Stone Age to Christianity,* (Garden City, 1957), pp. 271–272.

[13] Jos. 24, 2.

[14] What is uttered is not other than the divine nature itself, hence it has all the divine "attributes." As the usual trinitarian formulae assert, what is communicated is not other than the "substance," the *ousia* of God. Hence, the Word is of one and the same (and not merely of a like) substance as God, *homoousios, consubstantialis Patri.*

"procession" within himself if his "procession" towards us is to be really a procession or uttering *of himself* (rather than of something sent in place of himself). Conversely, what he communicated *to us* would not be himself unless that which is communicated came from (proceeded) from him *in himself*. Thus, the Word of God was not only "with God," but "the Word was God."[15]

It would be inexact, therefore, to suppose that the Christian *theos* is the same as the *Yahweh* of the Old Testament. To be sure, there is a sense in which they are the same, that is, they are one and the same reality. But the experience and the concept of God evolved from that of the Old to that of the New Testament. The revelation of Jesus was a new revelation of God, calling for a new and deeper faith. Henceforth God should not be understood as having the paradoxical qualities of transcending creation yet entering into communication with man. The very transcendence of God was affected. It no longer removed his own reality in himself from the reality of man's immediate experience. God was a transcendent *presence,* that is, he "lived in," was immanent within, all being, all existence and most particularly in all men. He continued to be the creator of man and of heaven and earth. But his creativity was not that of a *demiourgos,* or even that of a like artificer, so accomplished that he needed no material to fashion his work of art; it was but the converse of his free self-communication and, therefore, identical with his presence to being. (For the Christian God was distinguished not by having performed the spectacular feat of having hewn being out of nothing, but by the yet more wondrous fact that he created the world in his own presence, and in order freely to give to it himself.) Therefore, the creator of heaven and earth was now

[15] Jn. 1, 1.

experienced as a reality which, though "wholly other" than experience and existence, was closest to experience and most intimately related to existence.

Or perhaps it would be better to say that the *utter* transcendence of God was now revealed for the first time, its plenitude having been hidden from the Old Testament. For God's transcendence was no longer a separation between God and creation, an alienation bridged by his apparitions, messages and visitations. In the Christian conception of God there was no longer the slightest opposition between transcendence and immanence—for it was no longer a question of having to use contradictory categories to express *different* aspects of the same God. The Christian God is not *both* transcendent and immanent. He is a reality *other* than being who is *present* to being (by which presence he makes being to be). It is because he is *wholly* other, that his otherness cannot exclude presence to creation—otherwise he would be less than totally other, since to be excluded from creation he must share a common ground with it. In brief, God no longer "sent word" or "spoke" to us from on high. He now lived with us "here below," and shared our history, our humanity, our nature and our life. And so, "the Word was made flesh, and dwelt among us."[16]

Now, the word used by the author of the prologue to the Fourth Gospel to designate the Word which—proceeding from God yet not being other than God himself—must be said to *be* God, was *logos*. What is difficult for us to realize today is that what made this expression particularly apt to signify the Christian experience of the God who, as subsisting self-communication communicated himself to us in the person of Jesus, was not, as St. Thomas thought, the Word's similitude to a mental con-

[16] Jn. 1, 14.

cept or mental word, which proceeds "by way of emanation of the intellect."[17] True, the self-communication of God is like an utterance, insofar as that which is communicated emanates from God. But the Old Testament already knew as much. What distinguished the New Testament's revelation of God was not that the Word *is* like an utterance, which indeed it is, but that despite emanating from God it is *not* like an utterance in a very important respect: although the point would not be made fully clear until well after Nicaea, an integral part of the original Christian concept of God was that the consubstantiality of the Word with God did not merely mean that the Word was of a *like* nature (*homoiousios*) to that of God "the Father," but of one and the same nature (*homoousios*) with him. Insofar as *logos* meant simply "emanation of the intellect" the term was not particularly apt to signify the second person of the trinitarian Christian God.

But the term *logos* did not simply mean an "emanation of the intellect," or *speech, concept, word* (*sermo, verbum*); it also meant *reason* (*ratio*). But even this translation is misleading. *Logos* did not mean exclusively, or even primarily, the reason of man, the intellect. It meant primarily a more abstract reason; we might indeed call it a *rationality* which pervaded all reality, a rationality which the human intellect simply reflected inwardly and subsequently uttered to itself in concepts, which in turn were signifiable by spoken words. The Christian *logos,* to be sure, was no abstraction. But in religious and philosophical terminology *logos* had signified since Heraclitus's time, and especially in the thought of Philo Judaeus and in the Stoics, an intelligible reality within beings, yet distinct from them, which produced their intelligibility and reality. This *logos* did emanate from God, but

[17] *ST,* I, 34, 2.

its principal function was neither to mediate God's knowledge of himself, nor to make God known to us, nor even to reflect or communicate to us the intelligibility of things: its essential role was to make things intelligible and real. The *logos* was the immanent principle, "divine" in nature, which accounted for the reality, the origin, the existence, the dynamics, the order, the harmony and the meaningfulness of the world.

If we suppose this *Weltanschauung,* we should have little difficulty in understanding why the Fourth Gospel should tell us that the Word "was in the beginning with God; all things were made through him, and without him was not anything made that was made" (RSV). As adopted by Christian theology, and in the first place by the Fourth Gospel, *logos* did not merely signify the emanation of the Word from God, nor merely the Word's likeness to, or share in, the divine nature, nor indeed even the mere consubstantiality of the Son with God. It signified the consubstantiality of the *Incarnate* Word and God, for "the Word was made flesh." And *logos* signified this not by reason of its gnoseological, but of its metaphysical connotations. In short, if the God of Christian belief was the self-communicating God who revealed himself to man not only by sending messages, but also by being present to us in all things at all times, and ultimately most fully and completely by coming to us, to our experience, in person, "taking flesh," being born, sharing human nature, and dwelling in our midst, then the Christian God who revealed himself to us in the person of Jesus was in reality that which in hellenic usage was already—indeed, had traditionally been—called the *logos.* The philosophers had never realized it, but "the *logos* was God."

The distinctive idea of Christian theism, thus, was not that God was a unique and Supreme Being who entered into relations with us "here below." Christian theism elevated monotheism to the conception that God, though wholly other than any being, is a reality who *in his very reality* lives here below: the reality indeed whose inner reality in himself is to communicate himself to himself, in consequence of which he also communicates himself to us. Rather, this was only part of the distinctive idea of Christian theism, for there was a further aspect which followed on this.

God's self-communication *to* us has a certain consequence *in* us, namely, that when he communicates himself to us God then truly "lives" in us. More precisely, he lives in us effectively to the degree that his self-communication does effectively communicate—that is, to the degree that he is *received* by us. (Faith is, correspondingly, our acceptance, our letting-be of God's self-communication to us.) But the inspiration of God which is created in us by his self-communication is not the mere eliciting of a response. It is a true inhabitation by the true God himself—so that although the divinity residing and acting in us transcends the self-containment and uniqueness of God insofar as it proceeds from God,[18] that which inhabits in us is no other than God himself. God's inspiration in us, therefore, is God himself, *in his very reality,* made present to us by himself: and this is what is called the Holy Spirit. Now, the doctrine of the *threeness* or *trinity* of God is the affirmation that this religious experience "in" us reflects what is true of God "in" himself; that God truly is as he appears to us; that "God *stands in relation* [*verhält sich*] to the justified man as Father, Word, Spirit, and *is* this too, in and for himself."[19]

The theism of the New Testament goes so far beyond the Old

[18] And, to be sure, *filioque.*

[19] Rahner, *Theological Investigations,* I, p. 148. (Italics in the original.)

Testament monotheism which it so perfectly assumes, that its ultimate basis must actually be considered not as the *unicity* of God (monotheism) but the *self-communicating procession* of God ("trinitarianism"). The doctrine of God of the New Testament does not *begin* with the oneness of God, to which the concept of the three-persons-in-one-nature is *added* by way of modification. It begins with the procession of God. From this it follows that the oneness of the Christian God is *not* to be understood as a sort of extreme rarity, a rarity so great that it renders him unique in a splendid isolation. On the contrary, it is an abundance, indeed a *commonplaceness* so great as could pertain only to a *totally* transcendent reality, present to and in all things yet distinct from all severally and collectively. As Karl Rahner has put it (using the orthodox distinctions which emerged in order to conceptualize the foregoing): the New Testament doctrine of the Trinity "begins with the three Persons (three Persons, who are of a single divine nature) or better, with the Father, who is the source from which the Son, and through the Son the Spirit, proceed, so that the unity and integrity of the divine nature is conceptually a *consequence* of the fact that the Father communicates his whole nature."[20]

The concepts provided by the hellenic culture, especially that of the *logos* and those which led to distinction between *person* and *nature,* served admirably well to bring into full consciousness and to formulate the foregoing Christian faith in the Christian God. We have not to date managed to do *better*. On the other hand, this does not mean that the formulation of the doctrine in the hellenic terms of *word, nature* and *person* has not had serious disadvantages, even from early times, and increasingly so in more recent ages. We have *not managed* to do better. It is

[20] *Ibid.*, p. 146. (Italics in the original.)

because we have not done better since the fifth century that the future development of the doctrine of the Trinity must *begin* with Nicaea and Constantinople as from a point of departure. But it is because we *have not* managed to do better that we must *depart* therefrom and proceed forth. Moreover, we *must* depart. The doctrine of the Trinity, the absolutely basic doctrine of the Christian faith, has through undevelopment become inadequate to the point that it must be seriously suspected of causing some scandal—not simply that of incredibility but that of irrelevance and senselessness.

The contemporary inadequacy of conceptualizing the second person as the *Word,* for instance, should be fairly clear from what has been said above. There is nothing in our contemporary experience corresponding to the *logos* of the Greeks that could be fittingly or intelligibly called *Word.* To say that at the beginning of time the Word already was, and that the Word was God, should be most significant and important to someone who first assumes that there *is* a "Word." To someone who does not perceive the world by means of such a concept these propositions cannot reveal very much about God. On the contrary, they are likely to appear as cryptic utterances made by God concerning an unintelligible fact about himself. In any event, it is not simply a question of the concepts used to think of the various "persons" of the Trinity. There are more basic inadequacies concerning the concept of the *Trinity* as a whole. I will mention here only two ways in which conceptualizing the God of Christian belief in the hellenic form of trinitarianism has been disadvantageous, to the degree that this conceptualization was taken to be the final and substantially unchanging form of that belief.

The first made its appearance long ago. It consisted in that the formulation of the doctrine in the opposed concepts of nature and person—God is three consubstantial persons—automatically lent itself to understanding the Trinity as a sort of property of the divine nature: the position of the tract on the Trinity in St. Thomas's *Summa Theologiae* is symptomatic of this tendency.[21] In time, the Trinity became the doctrine of "one God in three persons." Thereafter the Christian concept of God no longer "begins with the three Persons"; it begins, at best, with the Lord of Hosts or, more likely, with the highest among the Platonic Forms, or with an Aristotelian unmoved Mover and First Cause, or with Subsisting Being Itself. At least, the theological and philosophical concept of God begins with one of these. Unavoidably planed down by less delicate handling than that which professional theologians and philosophers can afford,[22] these concepts have tended to become for the many in the Church the ordinary concept of God as the Supreme Being Who is the Ruler of the Universe—a Supreme Being who, *moreover* (a moreover which only supernatural revelation communicated), for some

21 "That which belongs to the unity of the divine essence having been considered, it remains to treat of . . . the Trinity," *ST*, I, 27, *prooemium*.

22 I do not mean that the Christian pedestrian's concept of God must necessarily be cruder than that of the Christian theoretician. I merely suggest that this happens unavoidably (and regrettably) once the concept of God is hellenized. For as it becomes hellenized it becomes metaphysical, and metaphysical thinking requires the training and education that only relatively few can afford. Under a different cultural form Christianity might once again make belief the fountainhead and inspiration of theo-logical speculation, not the other way about. This would entail, of course, a de-hellenization and a re-conceptualization of *enquiry, speculation* and *theory* so as to prevent their severance from common experience. The advantage of this follows from the facts that "in being knowers or thinkers we do not thereby cease to exist" and that "presence is not merely the object of speculative discourse; it is also the object of a speculative *existence*," (Hinners, p. 208). Christian theology and philosophy would then cease to be "academic" subjects, and theo-logical enquiry would once again take place predominantly within the public, everyday, real life of the whole Church.

inexplicable, mysterious reason happened to subsist in three personalities. In due course, the meaningfulness of the Trinity for the experience of faith in God, and the sense of the historicity of God's relations with man, had perforce to become attenuated as the eternity, immutability, self-sufficiency and aseity of the First Cause of being became the *fundamental* components of the concept of God. The concept of a "trinitarian" God personally involved in human events out of the abundance of his reality was bound to become gradually subordinated to that of a monotheistic Supreme Being eternally contemplating himself in heaven while keeping a tight rein on his refractory, restless subjects here below. Trinitarianism was effectively weakened into a modified monotheism.

The other disadvantage of the conceptualization of the Trinity in hellenic forms has not taken effect until more recently. If it is true, as suggested above, that the Christian God is not merely a transcendent and monotheistic God, but one who in the real presence of his reality to the reality of being unites transcendence and immanence—if it is true, thus, that the Christian experience of the trinitarian God transcends the monotheism of the Old Testament—the understanding of the Trinity as superimposed on the unity of the divine nature must ultimately lead not only to a weakening of trinitarianism into monotheism, but also to a weakening of monotheism itself.

As long as cultural contact was maintained (as it was during the middle ages) with the hellenism in which *natura, substantia* and *persona* were realities of common experience, the weakening of trinitarianism did not have noticeably ill effects. But in recent times the same condition has no longer obtained. *Person* has long ceased to mean *prosopon* or *persona,* and *personality* cannot today remotely convey the idea of a *mode of subsistence,* except perhaps to him who deliberately subtracted himself from contemporary experience and learned through long and arduous training to see the world as the mediaevals did. But to him who is formed by the twentieth century, *person* means (whether in reflexive or in merely lived awareness), a center of consciousness and, therefore, a center of *exercised* existence, life, presence, freedom and reality. A person is a being who does not merely *have* life and existence, but one who *exerts* himself towards life and existence; it is a being whose *being* is life and existence. A person, thus, cannot be a termination of nature. On the contrary, nature is a termination of personality—and a person, moreover, terminates itself and makes its nature in and through existing.[23]

The Christian believer of today, therefore, can repeat faithfully the formula: one God in three persons. But, (except as noted), in his actual and effective religious life he cannot very well avoid the thought that personality accounts for existence and nature, not vice versa, and that therefore three persons must be three beings, even if they all share one and the same substance and nature. The Trinity, therefore, is *effectively* conceived (however much one may subsequently deny to oneself the conception), as three distinct divine beings who somehow, mysteriously, make up one God. Our orthodox confessions of faith serve to hide the fact that the mass of Christians today are tempted to understand the Trinity as the mystery of three God-beings sharing a single divinity. In a word, we suffer from *crypto-tritheism*.[24]

The very conceptualization of the trinitarian God as God's *threeness* has contributed to this. The concept naturally emphasizes the *distinction* of persons rather than the *processions*

[23] Gabriel Marcel, *Being and Having,* (New York, 1965), pp. 154–174.
[24] Karl Rahner and Herbert Vorgrimler, *Theological Dictionary,* (New York, 1965), p. 472.

and the *self-communication* of God. No doubt, this emphasis was most useful at one point, in order to avoid that conception of God, at variance with Christian tradition, according to which the persons of God were but different modes in which he *successively* manifested himself (modalism). But the term *Trinity* now suffers from the opposite defect: it tends to obscure the fundamental Christian idea that God *does* manifest himself and that he does so precisely as Trinity; that his transcendence and immanence are not mysteriously irreconcilable aspects of him but, on the contrary, the result of his simple *presence* to being; and that the different persons *are* different modes (albeit not successive ones) of his self-communication. The bare dogma, *the Trinity of God,* no longer conveys—on the contrary, it tends to conceal—what is an integral and necessary part of the Christian concept of God, namely, that

> God's self-communication to his creature has been so absolute that the "immanent" Trinity (existing in God himself) is the "economic" (that which deals with men and brings about their salvation . . .). Conversely, the Trinity of God's dealing with us is already the reality of God as he is in himself: tri-"personality." From that experience of our faith which the Word of God himself . . . gives, we can therefore say that God's absolute self-communication to the world, *as* a mystery that has approached us, is in its ultimate originality called Father; *as* itself a principle acting in history, Son; *as* a gift bestowed on us and accepted, Holy Ghost. This "as", which is ordered to us, is really the self-communication of God "in himself"; the triplicity affirmed is thus a triplicity of God in himself. But since the communication of God is concerned in both cases (and not two effects that differ as creatures do), in both cases the "same" God is concerned.[25]

It should appear from the preceding that the Trinity and the Incarnation are not really two separate, successive "mysteries." The "trinitarian" conception of God begins with the belief that

[25] *Ibid.*, p. 471.

God communicates himself to us in the person of Jesus; it begins with the belief that Jesus is the Incarnation of God's "Word." Therefore, everything that has been said above of the dogma of the Trinity has a counterpart in the dogma of the Incarnation. But very brief remarks will suffice.

The belief that Jesus was not merely the "Christ," but indeed God's "Word," spelled the transformation of *Judaism* into *Universalism*. The Christ was essentially the redeemer of Israel. But the *Word* was the restorer of all things and all men. It was not simply that the Hebrew concepts of the "Son of man" and the "Holy One of Israel" could have had little appeal for mankind as a whole. The idea that Jesus was the Christ, but that the Christ was the *logos,* meant that man was redeemed by God himself in person, and not by mere man, however "holy" or however "sent" by God. The concept of the Incarnation of the Word, that is, the divinity of the Christ Jesus, could (in principle) be the focal point of the organization of all religious experience for every man, everywhere and at all times, whereas the Hebrew concept of the Messiah could scarcely have served the same purpose. Here too the adoption of hellenic forms fostered the catholicization of the Christian faith. Rather, it facilitated its *ecumenization*. For the universe of the planet Earth and of the one human race had not yet been discovered—not to speak of wider universes which we have but recently begun to suspect. But one may well wonder whether the universalization of Christianity today and in the immediate future—not to speak of the eventual christianization of outer space—can be reasonably entertained without the re-conceptualization and development of the dogma of the Incarnation.

To take but one particular aspect of it, casting the doctrine in the concept of the *hypostatic union*—the union of the two *natures,* the human and the divine, in the one divine *person* of the Word—may well have preserved orthodoxy and positively served to develop the Christian faith. But it may also have tended to stabilize Christian belief far too much. Of course, the idea that there could be too much dogmatic stability, that orthodoxy *requires* the development of dogma, has not occurred to the Christian mind until recent times—in fact, it is even today far from commonly accepted or, as yet, authoritatively taught in a consistent and unmystifying way. On the other hand, to the mind of the Fathers of Ephesus and Chalcedon orthodoxy and the stability of truth may have been very difficult to distinguish. The posthumous condemnation of Theodore of Mopsuestia, for instance, was required for the very sake of excluding possible avenues of development. The predominantly negative character of the traditional form of definitions, the *anathema sit,* illustrates this well. It is only today that we have begun to glimpse the possibility of profiting by encouraging exploration along divergent paths. Only today we can find complementary value in both Cyril and Theodore—largely because only today we can share the latter's anachronistic, non-hellenic, philosophical assumptions concerning eternity and time.

Meanwhile, since no Christian believer today (unless he can abstract himself from contemporary experience) can understand *suppositum* or *hypostasis* as the primary subject of existence, action and attribution, but only as the primary object of consciousness, it follows that no Christian believer today (except as noted) can intelligently believe that in the one *hypostasis* of Jesus *two* real natures are united. For us today, typically, subjectivity is not a center of being which is opposed to objectivity. Person (as subject) is a center of consciousness: it is that which can objectify itself. It is that which can objectively signify itself to itself by means of its (conceptual) self. Without personality, therefore, there can be no true humanity. If Jesus was able to think of himself as a human being, then he had a human personality. For a person is a being that can exist for-itself, that is, a being that can make its-self the object of experience and existence. A being cannot be human without knowing itself as human, nor can it know itself as human without being a man. If Jesus was unable to think of himself as a human being, to have a human consciousness—and, thus, to be a human person—then he was not a true human being. If, on the contrary, he was only a divine person, then he was not a true man.

To the same extent that contemporary man must tend to conceive personality thus, (and every member of the culture, even a Christian, shares to some degree the progressive self-consciousness which the philosopher, the scientist and other researchers professionally cultivate), the contemporary Christian must find it extraordinarily difficult to avoid the idea that if in Jesus there was only one person (namely, the divine person of the Word), then Jesus was not a human being at all. The doctrine that the only person of Jesus was that of the Word must really mean, however much we may deny it to ourselves, that Jesus was really God hiding under the appearances of being man.[26] But there could be in Jesus no human experience, no human consciousness, no human self-concept, for if there were he would be a human self.

The question of the reality of the temptations of Jesus is a touchstone. Likewise, we cannot easily allow Jesus any ignorance, any immaturity, any inexperience, any of the *normal* imperfec-

[26] At a very unsophisticated (but possibly not exceptionally rare) level of common opinion these appearances may even be restricted to his having a body.

tions which a being must have if his being is present to itself—we all but suppose that Jesus lying in the manger affected neuromuscular incoordination and an inability to talk. We are constantly tempted indeed to suppose that throughout his life Jesus chose to put on a thoroughly deceptive act. The best we can normally do today as we repeat the orthodox formulae is no longer to assume that Jesus was a man and believe he was God: it is to assume that he was God and believe he was a man. Or at least, to admit it. For we find it very difficult to follow through, and our imagination boggles, paradoxically, not at the divinity, but at the humanity of the Christ. In a word, we suffer from *crypto-docetism*.

THE RELATION OF SCHOLASTIC PHILOSOPHY TO MODERN ATHEISM

So far we have considered certain inadequacies of Christian theism resulting from the hellenization of the Christian faith. The hellenization of the Christian faith's speculation has produced certain parallel inadequacies in Catholic philosophical thought. The most obvious of these is not directly relevant to the question of theism and, therefore, will be but mentioned here. The Catholic's loyalty to his community should not blind him to the distressing fact that since the end of the middle ages Catholic philosophical thought has not produced very many contributions to man's understanding of himself or of reality. Its conception of knowledge of truth, of enquiry, of man, of change, of time, of reality, and even its conception of philosophy itself—all these conspire to deny Scholasticism the possibility of becoming so dissatisfied with its own real and valuable truth that it must consciously and intentionally seek to surpass itself. This is surely not unrelated to the yet more surprising fact that among the many theological developments that in recent times have facilitated and justified the renewal of the Church, and which continue to serve it, few if any have been inspired by Scholasticism. Insofar as Catholic theology today needs philosophy, it needs a philosophy that would not preclude *creative* development. It cannot be well served by a philosophy that permits no more than the eduction of act from potency. Creative Catholic theology has therefore increasingly turned to non-Scholastic (which means almost exclusively non-Catholic, indeed, non-Christian) philosophical thought. One can only hope that this unfortunate state of affairs will not continue indefinitely.

There is, however, another inadequacy of the traditional Catholic philosophy which is pertinent to our theme. I now refer to the hellenization of Christian philosophical speculation as constituting, in point of historical fact, the condition of the possibility of modern atheism. In this summary account I will restrict myself to bare fundamentals. It will make, nevertheless, a somewhat complex recital.

It is not by chance that the problem of the existence of God has been historically paralleled by the problem of the existence of objects of knowledge. To understand the connection between the two let us note that Greek philosophy and Scholasticism share a fundamental principle which makes them both "metaphysical." This is Parmenides' postulate of the equivalence of being and intelligibility.[27] The Greek metaphysical tradition which began with Plato and Aristotle never doubted the existence of intelligible reality or the reliability of knowledge, because in addition to the postulate of Parmenides it assumed that being existed necessarily—the Greek cultural experience would hardly

[27] "That which can be thought is identical with that which can be," *Fr.* 3, (Freeman trans.).

have permitted Greek philosophers to think otherwise. Scholasticism, however, adopted the Parmenidean principle, but consciously rejected (on account of its evident inconsistency with the Christian faith) the only condition that made it epistemologically viable, namely, the existential necessity of the actual as such.

For the Greeks the necessity of being meant the necessity of being *as such*. Evidently, they were not unaware that in a certain sense the beings of this material world are not necessary. But this only meant that the individual being was contingent insofar as it was material and potential. But every being *as such,* and not only the Supreme Being, was necessary. It was necessarily actual (that is, necessarily existing and necessarily intelligible), insofar as it participated in being, that is, precisely insofar as it was in act. For example, this individual *man* may be contingent precisely as individual, as concretized in matter. But *Man,* the species, is necessary, indeed eternal. For being as such, since it is necessary, is also eternal. Thus, although every individual being in the material world is subject to change and is in a sense contingent, for it has a beginning and an end, the world as a whole is necessary, eternal, unmoving and without beginning or end.

Now, like the Greeks, the Christian philosophers thought that the Supreme Being was necessary. But unlike the Greeks they could not countenance even the foregoing relative necessity of creatures: it is precisely as created *beings* that God's creatures must be totally contingent if the gratuitous self-communication of an utterly transcendent God is to be upheld. Pressed thus by Greek philosophy on the one side, and by the Christian faith on the other, Scholasticism sought to escape its dilemma with an ingeniously simple solution, namely, by restricting the necessity of creatures exclusively to their intelligibility, that is, to their *essence.* After Parmenides, Greek metaphysics had identified the necessity of being and the necessity of intelligibility through the identity of being and intelligibility. The Scholastics simply distinguished the necessity of intelligibility from that of being, so that a creature could have (as in Greek philosophy) a necessary intelligibility and nevertheless (as in the Christian faith) remain totally contingent precisely as being and as actual—the difficulty was that the Scholastics also retained the Parmenidean identification of being and intelligibility.

The story has been often and ably told of the metaphysical revolution that this simple solution entailed, and particularly the transformation of metaphysics itself from the science of being as *substance* (*ousia*) to that of being as *being,* properly so called. For our purposes, however, we need only note that the retrenchment of necessity to the bastion of essence implied the doctrine of the real distinction in creatures between *essence* and *existence.* For this was, indeed, the effect actually intended by the restriction of necessity to essence, namely, to make the *whole* actuality of the being of creatures totally contingent while nevertheless retaining the Parmenidean identity of being (and, therefore, of necessity) with intelligibility. But in God, of course, the opposite was required, since in him actuality and necessity should go together with each other and with intelligibility. In brief, the Scholastic modification of Greek metaphysics in order to bring it into line with the Christian faith, consisted in the twofold doctrine that (a) there is in creatures a real distinction between essence and existence, but (b) in God essence and existence are identically the same.

St. Thomas's doctrine to this effect is especially noteworthy not only because it was the first fully fledged, unequivocal and systematic expression of an elusive insight that Christian thinkers who assumed the Greek metaphysical outlook had long been reaching for, but also because it already included an explicit reference to the doctrine's epistemological implication, namely, the disgregation of essence and existence insofar as they are *knowable to us:* "Now, every essence or quiddity can be understood without anything being known of its existing . . . From this it is clear that the act of existing is other than essence or quiddity, unless, perhaps, there is a being whose quiddity is its very act of existing."[28]

Had St. Thomas retained the contingency of creatures but rejected the postulate of Parmenides, the history of philosophy would have been far different. Of course, this is arguing *per impossibile.* As it was, less than one hundred years after St. Thomas wrote as above, William of Ockham logically enough drew from it the view that it would be perfectly possible for us to have knowledge of an object that did not actually exist (if only God produced that knowledge in us).[29] If "every essence or quiddity can be understood without anything being known of its existing," no amount of knowledge about anything could possibly tell us whether it actually existed. How, then, do we ever know that anything actually exists? The answer matters less than the doubt it implies.

We still have to account, of course, for the fact that while the "extramental" existence of the things which provide the objects of our knowledge remains problematic, there can be no doubt that as "objects," that is, as known, they unquestionably exist "in the mind." Unfortunately, any sufficient efficient cause—God, if not the nature of the mind itself—is in principle capable of being pressed into service in order to account for the reality of essences precisely as known; that is, once the question arises

[28] St. Thomas, *De Ente et Essentia,* IV; Maurer trans., p. 46.
[29] *In Sententiarum,* II, 25.

it is always possible to account for the "objective reality" of ideas (as Descartes would refer to it in the third of his *Meditations*), by means of some agency other than a correlative "formal reality." If the "formal reality"—to adhere to Descartes' terminology—was not the exclusive and necessary "cause" of the "objective reality" of "ideas," if actually existing things were not *the only possible* extramental cause of knowledge, how could philosophy ever determine *which* was the actual extramental cause of knowledge? And if so, how could philosophy ever establish that "formal reality" actually existed? The ultimate epistemological consequence of the distinction between essence and existence was to render impossible in principle our knowledge of whether any given essence actually exists: it was to render impossibly problematic the actual existence of objects of knowledge.

Now, it is true that for St. Thomas the distinction between essence and existence did not apply to God. On the contrary, in God the two were absolutely one. It may well be asked, therefore, granted that the epistemological consequences described above concerning the problematic nature of the existence of creatures actually follow, what possible ill consequences could the real distinction of essence and existence *in creatures* have for our knowledge *of God,* since there is in him *no* distinction between the two? Well, it has this direct consequence: that unless the existence of God be demonstrable *from the identity of his essence and existence,* then the existence of God is as problematic as that of creatures. Indeed, it is doubly so, because whereas creatures, however problematic their existence, are in any event (if they exist) objects of possible empirical intuition, God (even if he exists) can in no event be the object of an empirical intuition—at least, not "here below"—since he is not in the first place a sensible being. Thus, even if the existence of creatures is granted, the existence of God remains insolubly problematic.

Why should this be so? Could we not deduce the existence of a necessary being, of a first efficient cause, etc., from the actual existence of contingent beings, of effects, etc.? The answer, as long as we continue to assume the Greek conception of knowledge as one being's intentional assimilation of, and unilateral union with, another, must be no. For the doctrine that there is in God *no real* distinction between essence and existence implies that nonetheless there is a *conceptual* distinction between them. We *cannot* empirically intuit the real indistinction of essence and existence in God. We *must* nonetheless conceive the two as distinct. There is, therefore, an unbridgeable difference between the way in which God is *in himself* and the way in which he is *in our knowledge*. Therefore, unless God were the object of empirical intuition, our concepts are *in principle* unable to make known to us the actual existence of God. For, as Kant was to conclude, since the conceptual distinction between God's essence and existence does by definition *not* correspond to a reality in God, every application of our concepts to a transcendent God who is not empirically intuitable is either an overt or a masked form of the ontological argument.

In other words, the ultimate epistemological consequence of the real distinction between essence and existence in creatures is to render the *intellect* incompetent for knowing the actual existence of *any* essence, be it created or uncreated, necessary or contingent. To grant the actual existence of creatures on the ground that, demonstrable or not, they are the objects of *sensible* intuition, helps philosophy not at all towards knowing the actual existence of God—unless perhaps we could know God's existence on the same ground, namely, that although it is *indemonstrable,* nevertheless the existence of God is the object of immediate, *empirical* intuition. But since this is not the case, we are left with the antecedent alone: the existence of God is rationally indemonstrable. This, to repeat, has for its starting point the position that, *as a reflexive analysis of our knowledge reveals,* there is in created being a real distinction between essence and existence: for the real distinction *follows* "from this," namely, that "every essence or quiddity can be understood without anything being known of its existing."[30]

[30] Elsewhere, principally in *Contra Gentiles,* II, 52, (but cf. *De Veritate,* VIII, 8, and *ST,* I, 44, 1), St. Thomas reaches the same conclusion, namely, the real distinction of essence and existence in creatures, from arguments assuming a different premise, namely, the identity of essence and existence in God. But obviously these arguments in turn assume the existence of God. It is doubtlessly true that *if* God exists and *if* his necessity is that of a self-subsisting being, then essence and existence are identical in him and him alone. But that there exists in actual reality a being corresponding to the concept of God as a self-subsisting being is hardly self-evident to us, as St. Thomas admits (*ST,* I, 2, 1, obj. 2 & reply). Therefore, these *a priori* arguments rest upon the *a posteriori* one given in *De Ente et Essentia.* Indeed, existence aside, the bare *concept* of God's necessity as that of a self-subsisting being is either an *a priori* one (as Descartes thought), or else it is *derived,* as in *De Ente et Essentia,* from the contingency of creatures understood as "*the fact that* the essence of a creature in no way implies its existence," (Maurer trans., p. 46; translator's annotation; italics mine). Moreover, even if, *per impossibile,* the *a priori* arguments did not rest upon the *a posteriori* one, this should not affect the conclusion I have reached, since they *assume* the existence of God and hence could not be admitted (as underlying the doctrine of the real distinction of essence and existence in creatures) for the purpose of attempting to demonstrate the existence of God in the light of the real distinction in creatures. Conversely, if (abstracting from God's actual existence) the *concept* of a God with identity of essence and existence did underlie the real distinction of essence and existence in creatures (and not the other way about), then every argument for the existence of God which would appear based on the contingent existence of creatures would surreptitiously introduce that identity into the argument. If so, every such argument would be a masked form of the ontological one—precisely as Kant observed.

The alternatives have been thoroughly explored during the fairly lengthy history of modern philosophy. Let us suppose, for instance, that we forget the above reasons which required Scholasticism to distinguish conceptually between God's essence and existence while denying the real distinction. The necessity of the conceptual distinction must nevertheless be maintained: the Arnauld-Malebranche controversy brought out a most important reason why. Not every one who knows that God exists thereby beholds God's essence: Christian philosophers allegedly know that God exists, and yet it could not very well be supposed that they enjoy the beatific vision. A distinction must therefore be made in *our* knowledge of God between his essence and his existence.

Whichever way we approach it, it is the conceptual distinction, not the real identity, that matters for philosophy's answer to the question whether God exists. The only alternative, in the absence of an empirical intuition of God, is to accept the validity of the ontological argument. But if *quoad nos* there is a necessary distinction between God's essence and his existence, it follows that his existence is problematic *in precisely the same way* as that of objects of knowledge, namely, because God's essence too "can be understood without anything being known of its existing." It was not, of course, until Descartes' failure to demonstrate the existence of God on the epistemological basis supplied by St. Thomas that the truth was driven home. But, unfortunately, by then there was no turning back.

But this is not all. St. Thomas had been able to demonstrate the existence of God because he had assumed that he, like everyone else, knew what God was. In his reasoning, it was necessary to arrive at a first mover, "and this everyone understands to be God"; it was necessary to admit that there existed a first efficient cause "to which everyone gives the name of God"; there must in actual reality be a necessary being, and "this all men speak of as God"—and so on, for a total of five times.[31] In the ripeness of philosophy's age, however, it became impossible to ask the question "whether God exists" without taking account of the consequences of saying that "essence can be understood without anything being known of its existing." The problem then became: to prove the existence of a God whose essence was unknowable to us yet whose concept was in point of fact possessed by everyone. But, as Descartes unwittingly showed, no one who did not already believe in God found it possible to solve this conundrum. Agnosticism, even by those who *believed* in God, was the philosophical conclusion to which this road logically led. More precisely, it was either the skepticism of unbelievers, or the fideism of Christians.

On the other hand, those to whom fideism was unacceptable, among them Catholics, because it was unreasonable, yet unlike Catholics were unwilling both to reject fideism and to *believe* that God's existence was demonstrable, found it logical to take the final step from skepticism and agnosticism to atheism. For, like "everyone," they too found themselves, though not immediately aware that God actually existed, possessed of a concept of God. The merely *agnostic* doubt hinged on the possibility that an actual reality might correspond to "that which everyone understands to be God." But if, upon investigation, this concept of God could be accounted for (for example, as by Marx or by Freud) as being produced by man himself out of his own resources, then the religious fact, as M. Garaudy has put it in the work quoted above, is reducible to the human fact. One must then deny the *reasonableness* of believing in God or of supposing

[31] *ST,* I, 2, 3.

that he might exist, for one has accounted for every human experience and still found no God. We might at this point recall the lapidary remark made by Laplace to Napoleon when the latter enquired about the role of God in the *System of the World:* "Sire," Laplace replied, "I have had no need for this hypothesis." "But it was not Laplace's *System*," Alexandre Koyré has commented, "it was the world described in it that no longer needed the hypothesis God."[32] In point of fact, it was not only the world scientifically described by Laplace that no longer needed it. God had also become superfluous for the Christian world in which Laplace lived.

I do not suggest that between St. Thomas and Karl Marx there runs a straight line. But I do suspect that the two can be joined by an unbroken one. Marcel Reding,[33] among other recent authors, has already suggested the filiation of Marxism to Aristotelianism. But the specific role of Scholastic metaphysics in this process—a role which was played only within the larger process of the generation of Marxism wholly from within Christianity—should be closely researched. It may also be pertinent to note in this connection that from this interpretation of history emerges the criticism of classical Marxism as a largely abortive effort among several "more or less vigorous attempts to escape from the Greek-Medieval tradition of *philo-sophia*." This criticism has been formulated by Richard Hinners in a passage so penetrating and succinct that I quote it in full:

Though Marxism is a justifiable reaction against idealism, yet it is an incomplete reaction since the root of idealism, the Greek speculative faith, is not uncovered and understood. The incompleteness of

[32] Alexandre Koyré, *From the Closed World to the Infinite Universe,* (Baltimore, 1957), p. 276.

[33] *Der Politische Atheismus,* (Cologne, 1957); *Marxismus-Leninismus, Geschichte und Gestalt,* (Berlin, 1961).

the Marxist reaction to idealism stems from interpreting the history of philosophy backwards from Hegel to the Greeks instead of forward from the Greeks to Hegel. This limitation means that matter, which is every bit as philo-sophical and speculative-ideological a concept as mind, becomes a speculable element within an ideological metaphysics and human existence and history become subjected to it. Marxism is not radical enough: it is not enough to overcome idealism. It is also necessary to overcome metaphysics as a speculative ideology.[34]

Likewise, I might add, the relative atheism of Marxism is not radical enough. For it is not enough to overcome the absolute theism of historical Christianity. It is also necessary to overcome the speculative-ideological metaphysics from which that absolute theism stems.

In any event, a token of the correctness of the thesis that Scholasticism provided the condition of the possibility of modern atheism, is the historical inability of Christian philosophical speculation in its Scholastic form to solve the antinomy of fideism and rationalism (which may not be unrelated to its more general inability to solve the antinomy between reason and revelation). Now, the nineteenth-century magisterium was not only persuaded, on the strength of the Christian faith, that fideism conflicted with the Christian tradition of concern with the truth of belief; it was also convinced, having accepted Scholasticism as the only proper form of Christian philosophical speculation, that the problem of the existence of God had been posed by the middle ages with perennial correctness—even if the modern answers to it, skepticism and atheism, were obviously unacceptable to the Christian faith (and were therefore to be accounted for as a historical perversion of philosophy). Vatican I's conclusion was the only logical one: it is a matter of *faith* that the existence of God is *rationally* demonstrable. Now, as a con-

[34] *Ideology and Analysis,* p. 131.

demnation of fideism this teaching is unquestionably in line with the Christian tradition. But in the history of ideas it can only be viewed as an unacknowledged admission of Scholasticism's inability to fulfill its own objectives and effectively demonstrate the existence of God. To repeat, as a condemnation of fideism the doctrine was unexceptionable. But the upholding of Scholasticism was superfluous and self-contradictory. For there is no intrinsic need for the Christian faith to assume the Scholastic mode of philosophizing about God. And a philosophy that had become so impotent that it needed upholding by faith should perhaps have been considered more of a hindrance than a help.[35]

It would lie outside the scope of this essay to offer a full-fledged alternative suggestion, more appropriate for our own day, to the Scholastic system of philosophical speculation about God. But it may be expedient to indicate parenthetically the general orientation one such alternative might take. Other aspects of it may be easily gathered from remarks already made and from those that will follow in the next chapter.

Perhaps the most significant defining point of an adequate

[35] The context should make clear that this remark applies not to mediaeval Scholasticism as such, but to its retention as the immutable form of Christian philosophy long after its time had passed. All I have said above about the positive benefits of Christianity's hellenization I believe to be applicable, with added emphasis, to its principal philosophical component, namely, medieval Scholasticism. But by the same token, the obsolescence of Scholasticism goes together with that of Christianity's hellenic cultural form. As human consciousness continued to develop beyond the middle ages (thanks indeed to its development *during* the Middle Ages) the usefulness of Scholasticism waned—at the same time that its employment gradually became its adoption in the sixteenth century, then its establishment early in the nineteenth, its beatification in 1879, and finally its canonization in 1917.

contemporary Christian philosophy (in general, but with special reference to its study of God) would be that it should *begin* with a consideration of the needs of the Christian faith, not those of Greek metaphysics. This means that it would feel free to disregard Parmenides' postulate and the Greek conception of knowledge as intentional intussusception and unilateral union of a knowing subject with an object of knowledge. The problem of God would then not have to be posed in terms of demonstrating the existence of God in abstraction from his nature. For if, in the first place, the *Christian faith* were concerned with the existence of God abstracted from his nature, it would presuppose a concept of God that would in one way or another (as St. Thomas imagined) depend upon our sole powers of knowledge. As we have seen, it would matter little, once we did so, whether our concept of God originated in an "innate" disposition (Descartes) or in the "pretensions" of an imperfect human intellect (Kant). Any such alternative would leave us free to believe in God, but it would also require us to affirm that God does not reveal *himself* to *our experience*. I stress both *himself* and *our experience,* for God would remain free to send us cryptic *messages* about himself—for instance, that he is three persons. These messages would of necessity be cryptic, because they could not communicate to *our experience* anything of God *himself*.[36] If, on the other hand, faith concerned a revealed

[36] At least in the popular faith of the Church revelation has indeed tended to become God's transmission of cryptic messages. Correlatively, the magisterium of the Church has tended to become the decoding of these messages, and faith the Christian's assent to the accuracy of the translation—this assent being warranted by the further beliefs that the original message was truly sent by God to the magisterium, and that the decoding is infallibly guaranteed by God. But since these further beliefs are themselves proposed by the magisterium, Christian belief has tended to become a vicious circle: we believe that Scripture is revealed

concept of God, faith in the existence of God would be superfluous, because it would be superseded by self-evidence. For God's revelation of *any* concept of himself would make his existence *as revealer* an empirical fact: the fact of his existence would be actually contained in the experience that such-and-such a concept of God was being revealed by God.

But we need not choose between believing in God's existence (as contrasted with his essence) or in his nature (as contrasted with his existence): the first article of the Christian creed indicates why. For the creed does not affirm "I believe that God [that is, a being whose concept is hereby presupposed] actually exists"; nor "I believe that God [that is, a being whose existence is hereby presupposed] is truthfully to be attributed such-and-such notes, to the exclusion of these others."[37] The creed's affirmation, "I believe in God,"[38] bears upon a simple reality, the reality of God, which cannot be analyzed into distinct aspects, however much the real unity of these aspects be thereafter asserted,

---

because we first believe the magisterium, which so teaches, whose truthfulness is guaranteed by the truth of the scriptural revelation in which we believe.

[37] To be sure, other propositions of the creed express some historically important ways in which the concept of God already affirmed by Christian belief was to be distinguished from, for example, those of paganism, gnosticism, etc. But however proper and true, these propositions do not express what God is. They qualify and distinguish what is conveyed in the first place by the concept *God*.

[38] The statement stands even if the first article of the creed is "I believe in *one* God." Here too *one* qualifies God (in the same way as "maker of heaven and earth") insofar as it refers to monotheism, that is, to belief in a God of which there is only one. But as I have noted above, the God of the New Testament goes beyond monotheism to "trinitarianism," and in this sense the formula means not simply "the God of which there is only one," but above all "the *true* God," "the only God who truly is God." In this sense, *unum* adds nothing but emphasis to *Deum;* it means the same as *God*.

without distorting the meaning of the belief. The totality and unity of this affirmation is rendered either impossible or unreasonable as long as the act of faith is made to bear upon the separate concepts of "God" and "existence."

From this it follows that the Christian's act of faith cannot consist in assenting to the proposition "I believe in God"; though he cannot very well have Christian faith without actually conceptualizing his belief (and, therefore, expressing it, at least to himself) in some such proposition as "I believe in God." But belief must bear *directly* upon the reality of God, not upon words or upon concepts;[39] this is the corollary to the idea that God

[39] I stress that faith must bear *directly* on the reality of God, in order to distinguish this from the doctrine of St. Thomas, *ST*, II–II, 1, 2, ad. 2, according to which faith *terminates* at God himself through the mediation of the propositions of the creed, but which nevertheless implies that belief bears directly on propositions about God. For faith is understood by St. Thomas as "to think with assent" (II–II, 2, 1) an object which "as regards the thing itself which is believed . . . [is God, but which] on the part of the believer . . . is . . . a proposition," (II–II, 1, 2). But this means that what we really assent to, and therefore what we really believe in (that is, what we really become *cognitively* related to) in the act of faith is not God, but the propositions of the creed: when the act of faith is "considered on the part of the intellect" faith can be described as "to believe in [an object who is] God, [*credere Deum*]," if considered in relation to the "material object" of faith, or as "to believe God, [*credere Deo*]," if considered in relation to "the nature of the formal object," (II–II, 2, 3). But the expression "formal object" has in this context a highly unusual meaning: it means "the medium on account of which such and such objects of belief are assented to, [*formalis ratio objecti, quod est sicut medium propter quod tali credibili assentitur*]," (*ibid.*). We return, therefore, to the idea that what we really assent to are the propositions about God. It remains true, of course, that faith can also be described as "to believe in God, [*credere in Deum*]," (*ibid.*), but this does not change the conclusion I have drawn, since faith can be so described only "insofar as the intellect is moved by the will" in the act of faith. In brief, St. Thomas's doctrine is that belief *in the propositions* of the creed *amounts to* belief *in God himself,* because the propositions of the creed are true—and a true proposition is one which

reveals himself, not words about or concepts of himself. Thus, the bearing of the faith upon the *reality* of God (and, consequently, its total and unitary character) cannot be reasonably and consistently maintained unless the affirmation "I believe in God" (and, *a fortiori,* the affirmations "God exists" and "God is such-and-such") are understood as the *conceptualization, culturally and historically conditioned,* of the Christian religious experience of belief in God.

But is it possible to transcend the conceptual dichotomy of God's essence and existence? Are we not bound by both the *nature* of our minds and the *nature* of reality conceptually to distinguish between the existence and the nature of God? I believe that it is possible to transcend it, that we are not by nature bound to it, any more than we are bound to affirm the real distinction of essence and existence in creatures in order to conceptualize their contingency. If we depart from Greek metaphysics at their Parmenidean root, knowledge is no longer an immaterial "intussusception" of reality, and the investigation of being is no longer guided by the equivalence of intelligibility

---

by virtue of its representative power bridges intentionally the ontological gap between object and subject. Obviously, this is a pre-critical understanding of belief.

On the other hand, the implication of the concept of faith suggested here is not that Christian belief consists in experiencing God "without concepts" in some mystical, immanentist or other extraordinary cognitive union. For the theory of knowledge assumed here does not understand concepts as the ordinary means of uniting subject and object, since it does not in the first instance understand knowledge as an intentional union of object and subject. Hence, the idea that belief must bear directly upon God's reality does not make of faith an extraordinary mode of consciousness: *all* consciousness bears directly upon reality. Conversely, it does not mean that faith, unlike other modes of consciousness, occurs "without concepts": *all* human consciousness is conceptual. But concepts are the necessary form of faith, as they are the necessary cultural form of all consciousness.

and being. Hence the contingency of creatures would not be conceived as a real distinction between essence and existence, but as that peculiar quality of their factuality which consists in their appearing, their coming-into-being, their sudden emergence, as it were, onto the cosmic stage without having been previously listed in the program. (In this conception, evidently, essences are not possibly-existing divine ideas.) In man, where we first discover it, contingency is likewise the quality of his factual reality which requires him to appear to himself, to come-into-being in-and-for-himself, to make up his own role as he is suddenly pushed onto the stage of life. In other words, man's contingency is the fact that in order to be he must create himself.

It follows that in this view ontological enquiry would no longer be the investigation of *being as such*—whether in the Aristotelian or the Thomistic meaning of the words, that is, whether they mean being as *ousia* or whether they mean being as essentially related to (actual or possible) real existence. It would be no more and no less than the study of reality as such, that is, without abstraction from its reality, concreteness, immediacy, actuality, historicity and factuality. Thus, the dichotomy of essence and existence is not transcended specifically in relation to God. A "metaphysics of presence" such as Gabriel Marcel's, or an "eschatological metaphysics" such as Berdyaev's, do not conceive any reality as polarized by existence and essence. They are concerned with being in its empirical immediacy: they try to avoid every *a priori* construction such as that required to distinguish between essence and existence *as constituents of reality as such*.

Finally, with a theory of knowledge that would permit a distinction between religious experience and its conceptualization (such as that proposed in the previous chapter), a reasonable justification for believing in a revealed God would not be an impossible undertaking. For such a philosophy would not be concerned with demonstrating that a God whom "everyone" knows actually exists, or that God, a possible being and an actual object of knowledge, "objectively" exists. It would be concerned with showing how God himself *in his reality* is *present* to human experience. Its concern would be the presence and reality of God. Such a God, however, would not be even partially that of Greek metaphysics. For this would be an integrally *Christian* philosophy. Its God would be wholly and exclusively the Christian God.

5.

The Development of Christian Theism

For all the unwarranted and inexpedient inadequacies of the Christian faith today, and for all the underdevelopment of its theism, what is most typical of the present moment of Christianity is not that it suffers from these, by now inveterate inadequacies, but that the suffering has become acutely painful and threatens to become unbearable. This is the sign of fundamental health at the core of the Church. It reveals a heightening of self-consciousness, and where there is self-consciousness there is hope. Of course, not every Catholic would agree with the analyses suggested here, but the need for proper medication is fairly commonly avowed. On the working assumption of the diagnosis made above, that Christianity suffers from absolute theism, the question arises: Once Christianity becomes fully conscious of the need for further developing its theism, how is it likely to reconceptualize consciously its belief in God?

Nowhere in this essay would I want to stress the tentative and exploratory character of my remarks more than in my attempt to answer this question. All history, but very specially perhaps Christian history, is freely and spontaneously made by the creative forces generated by man's interrelations with the ultimate reality, God. For this reason history is radically unforeseeable.

Nevertheless, what is radically unforeseeable may well be empirically predictable: though we may not say what final goal we are bound to arrive at, we can determine in which direction we are already going. We can forecast what points we are likely to traverse, on the basis of the decisions we have already taken and on the assumption that we will follow them through.

I will not deal here with Protestant Christianity, a subject apart. But the Catholic Church in recent years has freely taken certain basic decisions which, to be sure, are in principle reversible, but which for the present remain a defining point of its orientation. The principal one was manifested most clearly, perhaps, in the general acceptance by the Church of the directive contained in Pope John's opening address to Vatican II. It was the decision to adopt a historical perspective: to "look to the present, to new conditions and new forms of life . . . to dedicate ourselves with an earnest will and without fear to that work which our era demands of us."[1] In the single moment of unhesitating acclamation with which this proposal was greeted—even if not a few among those who subscribed it were possibly not fully conscious of its ultimate import—the reversal took place of a policy which Christianity unconsciously began to develop at some time between the days of patristic hellenism and the age of medieval Scholasticism, and which had been implicitly espoused since the beginning of the sixteenth century and consciously abided by since the end of the eighteenth. This policy was, for the sake of protecting the truth and purity of the Christian faith, to resist the factual reality, and to deny the moral validity, of the historical development of man's self-consciousness, especially as revealed in cultural evolution. In the person of John XXIII the Catholic Church made an act of faith in the precisely opposite idea: that the truth of Christianity needs for

[1] *The Toronto Globe and Mail,* October 12, 1962.

its health, protection and development the reality of man's individual and cultural growth in self-consciousness. Despite hesitations and misgivings that have abounded as the implications of this act of faith have come to light, this remains for the present the Church's most fundamental principle of self-guidance—and, as we all sense, one which could not now be forsworn without the certainty of disaster.

In relation to the Christian faith in God it is not difficult to ascertain in principle what will be the consequence of this historic decision: it will be the remedying of the Christian faith's unwarranted and inexpedient inadequacy. This remedy should in turn mean, in negative terms, the conscious rejection of every form of absolute theism. It should mean, in positive terms, at first the restoration, and ultimately the deepening and perfecting of, the relative theism which inspires the Christian faith.

But how will this be manifested? How are we likely to conceive God—rather, in what way is our conception of God likely to shift—as these changes take effect? This is much more difficult to discern. In order to avoid in what follows the constant qualification that would be required as one attempted to answer these questions, I will stress at this point once for all the highly tentative and exploratory nature which speculation on the matter must necessarily have. We now stand on a very uncertain terrain. We are justified in exploring it solely for the attempt's possible heuristic value.

THE BEING AND EXISTENCE OF GOD

The Christian theism of the future might not conceive God as *a being*. I place the stress not merely on the indeterminate article *a* but also on the substantive *being*. In Scholastic philosophy God is not conceived as *a* being, but he is nevertheless conceived as *being* (*ens*). We might eventually go beyond this as well, if the methodological principle which may be operative in our future concept of God should transcend that which in Greek and, later, in Christian thought has always been at work. I refer again to the *metaphysical* method which rests on Parmenides' postulate of the convertibility of being and intelligibility. If reality is not assumed to be constituted by intelligibility—or by any (possible or actual) relation to mind[2]—reality can no longer be identified with that-which-is (which is the usual meaning of *being, ens*). To be sure, reality will still be as a matter of fact intelligible. But its intelligibility will now be a matter of *fact,* not of *necessity*. Being is intelligible, but not *as such*. Things can be understood, and can be conceived as being, because if they in fact exist they will also have a history—and this history makes them relatable to mind. Essences, therefore, what things are, are always created, whether created by another or self-created (in the case of consciousness).

Thus, man is most truly a being, because he is present to himself as an object. Transcending the subjectivity of mere objects and the objectivity of mere subjects, he understands himself as being. His transcendence, his spirituality, consists in being conscious and thus being able to be whatever he makes himself to be.[3] On the other hand, the open background against which he becomes conscious of transcendence and which is grasped in

[2] I stipulate the latter because in the philosophy of Sartre and certain other existentialists there is a confusion between the *neutrality* of being, as it were, with relation to mind (I mean, the mere *non-mental* character of reality as such), and its supposed *absurdity*. In this confusion we find the last refuge of the Parmenidean principle of mind-being equivalence. Sartre's transcendence of realism-idealism is less radical than he imagines. To understand reality as absurd is to understand it as intrinsically related to mind (albeit by a relation of mutual exclusion).

[3] Marcel, *Homo Viator,* pp. 13–28.

that empirical attitude which permits faith to emerge, is precisely that which is beyond man, beyond transcendence, and therefore beyond being. In Christian language this is called the uncreatedness of God. Well, then, the Christian must believe that God is uncreated. God cannot be created, whether by another or by himself. He should therefore not be conceived as being.

It should be made clear that this proposition is to be taken literally. Since the method which produces it is not that of Scholasticism, it does *not* mean this: that since God must in some real sense be a being because otherwise he would be nothing, yet he cannot be univocally said to be a being, we must *both* affirm and deny being of him, so that the proposition "God is not a being" really means "God is a super-being." What it means is literally what it says, that God is not a being at all. What the religious experience of God discloses is a reality *beyond* being. Nor do I suggest that if God is beyond being he is empirically unknowable, or that he is (unless we use the term hyperbolically) ineffable. Nor does saying that God is a reality beyond being mean that he can be experienced only mystically or through affective knowledge or connaturality. For unless we retain the Greek metaphysical outlook, the ordinary facts of Christian experience are sufficient to establish that we do *experience* God, but that we do not experience him as *being*. This proposition should be obvious and commonplace to the philosophically unprejudiced Christian believer. In fact, since it is a matter of simple observation it should be one of the starting points of a Christian philosophical enquiry that would rise to the empirical level of methodology to which philosophy has been developed in our time. We should determine what consequences for our understanding of God follow from this observation, rather than the consequences for our understanding of faith, within the general presuppositions of the Greek theories of knowledge, that follow from the presupposition that the God in whom we believe is the Supreme Being. God is, among other ways in which we can conceptualize the matter, that which we experience as the open background of consciousness and being. There is no need, if we discard Parmenides, to make God fit the mould of being (and afterwards say that the mould is really an Procrustean bed of analogical being). On the contrary, what we must do is to open ourselves to that which transcendence reveals.

By the same token, God cannot be said to exist. But there are two things which are *not* meant by this proposition. The first thing it does not mean is this: that although actually "God exists," this proposition must be complemented by its opposite, "God does not exist," in order to signify that the existence of God is only analogous to that of creatures, and that therefore "God, who does not exist, super-exists." The second thing it does not mean is this: that there is no reality transcending our experience of totality or of being, or that reality is exhausted by being, or that the openness of human transcendence is only a logical void, filled not by any reality but by nothing.

The reason why the latter construction should be rejected will appear as the positive aspect of this concept of God, namely, his *presence,* is developed below. But we can anticipate part of it. The affirmation that "God does not exist at all" takes nothing away from God's reality and presence. For *to exist* and to be *present* are quite different things. As Marcel has remarked, "we could say that the man sitting beside us was in the same room as ourselves, but that he was not really *present* there, that his *presence* did not make itself felt."[4] Conversely, God's real presence to us

[4] *The Mystery of Being,* I, p. 205.

(and, therefore, his reality "in himself") does not depend upon his being a being or an object. In fact, our belief in the Christian God is post-primitive to the degree that we apprehend that although there is no super-being behind beings, no supreme being who stands at the summit of the hierarchy of being, nevertheless a reality beyond the totality of being reveals itself by its *presence*. There can be, beyond the totality of all actually existing being, something *present* to us in our experience, in the sense that "when somebody's presence does really make itself felt . . . it reveals me to myself, it makes me more fully myself than I should be if I were not exposed to its impact."[5] The reality of human transcendence discloses the presence of a reality beyond all actual and possible empirical intuition, *if* in the presence of myself to myself I find that over and above my own agency (and indeed as the ultimate condition of the possibility of that agency) there is a presence which "reveals me to myself" in a supererogatory and gratuitous way, that is, by making me "more fully myself than I should be if I were not exposed to its impact."[6]

[5] *Ibid.*

[6] This, which is the only valid "proof" for the "existence" of God that I know of, I take to incorporate all that which seems valid in Maritain's "sixth way," *Approaches to God,* (London, 1955), pp. 62–65. I estimate, however, that Maritain's insight (that "the operations of the human intellect . . . [which] emanate from a subject or from a person" reveal by their self-insufficiency the existence of their source, God), is fundamentally voided by his confusion of God's *presence* with God's *sufficient causality*. It is therefore also marred by his consequent conceptualization of God as that in which the thinking self "pre-existed" or "existed before itself in a first existence distinct from every temporal existence." In point of fact, the question of *priority* and *posteriority,* metaphysical or otherwise, does not enter into it any more than does *causality*. On the contrary, the presence of God does not exhibit him as a prior, anterior, supra-temporal or eternal reality: it manifests him as a *present* one. The

The other construction of the original assertion above is to be rejected because as a means of developing the Christian concept of God the method of analogical predication is no longer useful. Its true value has been limited and negative, namely, to have enabled Christian thought to preserve a *faith* in God's transcendence while *reasoning* about him as if he were not transcendent. The method has not and could not have enabled philosophy to *conceive* and *understand* God in an essentially more adequate way than was possible to Greek metaphysics. It has enabled Scholastic philosophy merely to *acknowledge* the inadequacy of its hellenic conception of God—or, rather, to admit it without consciously acknowledging it. When analogy has been used well, it has served to introduce a qualification to every positive statement about God, a qualification which, once made, philosophy could proceed to ignore. And even this limited value has been lost whenever it has been mistaken for an actual means whereby to make empirical concepts perform a role they cannot otherwise perform. Thus, the proposition that "God does not exist" (in the Scholastic sense) has sometimes served to *hide* the insufficiency of the proposition that "God exists"—which is the one that has been really operative. In other words, when philosophy follows this method it only *says* that it provides a *meta*-physical understanding of God: it only *says* that it describes God *per*

---

point can hardly be missed once we rid ourselves of any hellenic compulsion to think of God as the First (or the Last) Cause, or as the *arche* and *aitia* of existence, or as the Supreme Being.

I should underline that the "proof" I have suggested above not only has nothing to say about God's "existence" properly so called, but that it is hardly a proof in the classical sense of the term. It concerns a reality which is not the object of any actual or possible empirical intuition. Therefore, it is an essentially *unverifiable* argument. It is always possible to look at the same facts and find nothing but the *absence* of God. This is why I have formulated the argument in hypothetical form.

viam remotionis et eminentiae. The method is rightly called analogical *predication.* It does not provide analogical *understanding.* It only provides a conception of God in strictly "physical," human terms which is modified by the (implicit) *statement* that these terms are inadequate.[7] It is true, of course, that the terms of the traditional Scholastic conception of God are inadequate; but Scholastics unduly attribute this inadequacy to their positive, empirical nature or to their human character. We can philosophically account for man's experience of

[7] The doctrine of analogy is the logical outcome of attempting to explain how we can conceive God while holding simultaneously (a) that knowledge is an intentional intussusception through the means of concepts, (b) that all our concepts are derived from empirical intuition, and (c) that God is not, at least "here below," known to us by any empirical intuition. The solution consists in supposing that concepts derived from empirical intuition *can* adequately reach an object beyond empirical intuition if only we recognize, avow and state that such concepts *cannot* adequately reach an object beyond empirical intuition.

The key assumption is, of course, the first. In a theory of knowledge in which human cognition is not an intussusception but a relational existing-with which results from the self-differentiation of consciousness, all our concepts are derived from empirical intuition. God can be adequately conceived by us in the concepts of empirical intuition because he is experienced by us as a reality given *in* empirical intuition. But since he is not an object of thought or a being, the experience of God is the experience of an inevident reality. Hence, the experience is, however "rational" and reasonable, an experience of the order of *belief.* Conversely, belief in God is, however inevident, contingent and gratuitous, neither supra-rational nor infra-empirical. It is an experience in essentially the same fundamental sense as any other: when we believe in God we *experience* him. This means that although God is not an *object* of empirical intuition, his self-communicating reality (that is, his-self as rendering itself *present* to us) is experienced by us *in* the empirical intuition of objects, principally and most immediately in the empirical intuition of consciousness, selfhood and existence as objects of thought. This is why the experience of God takes on the peculiar character of *faith;* it is also the reason why the reasonableness and correctness of any "demonstration" of the reality of God does not take away the need to believe in God if one is to *experience* and *know* him at all.

God in terms which are not intrinsically inadequate, if we first account for human experience in more adequate terms than Scholasticism does.

The proposition that "God cannot be said to exist" can be properly and literally understood by the Christian believer in God, on the grounds that *to exist* (in the literal sense of the term, *to arise out of, to emerge*), is proper to a being, that is, to that which is created or creates itself and is, therefore, a thing (*res*), a that-which-has-essence. If God is not a *res* and if he has no essence, then he does not exist. To attribute existence to God is the most extreme form of anthropomorphism. This anthropomorphism Christian philosophy has had to indulge only because of the inability of hellenic metaphysical thinking to discern *reality* except in *ens,* that-which-is. To be sure, the Christian experience of God *can* be cast in the concept of being. It can also be cast, however, in the concept of reality, as the presence of that which (though not itself being) manifests itself in and through being, that-which-is. That-which-exists is *as such* a manifestation of God. But it is not God himself.

The idea that God should not be conceived as existing incorporates, but goes beyond, the attempt of some contemporary Catholic thinkers, notably Gilson, to conceive God as "beyond essence," but nonetheless as "subsisting existence itself." The insight that "God has no essence," that "God is as a beyond-essence,"[8] is valid. But it must be taken seriously and followed through. It means, among other things, that the reality of God does not have an *objective* meaning. God does not have meaning in-and-for-himself, though he can have, of course, meaning for-us. For meaning is essentially relative; it is always given-and-

[8] Gilson, *Elements,* p. 133.

received. But the transcendence of God goes together with his uncreatedness. He can be given meaning by us in order to be conceived and understood and, conversely, we can receive the meaning which he makes himself have for us and gives to us (that is, his self-revelation). But he could not give meaning to himself (in order to be) unless he were, like man, self-created. Hence he cannot be a pure-existence-beyond-essence. The self-creation of Hegel's Absolute Spirit is the final consequence of conceiving God as *ens;* and to conceive God as an *ens* whose essence is to be *and hence has no essence,* is only but one step removed from Hegel. Why, then, does Gilson not take that step? The exploration of this question should help us understand the difference between his view of God and that suggested here.

Up to a point the basis of Gilson's position is the same as the one I have suggested above. Since essence, he writes, is "proper to the being of creatures, we must give up essence [in our attempt to understand God] in order to reach the open sea of pure actual existence."[9] But the difference between this doctrine and what I have said above (and therefore the reason why Gilson cannot follow through the doctrine that God has no essence) should be evident from the fact that immediately he adds: "but we must also keep the notion of essence present to mind so as not to leave it without any object." Gilson must add this qualification to his previous denial of God's essence because as long as one adopts the principle of Parmenides one cannot understand reality except in the correlative (but, after the Thomistic modification, mutually exclusive) concepts of essence and existence.

But this means that there is an inconsistency in Gilson's position. The doctrine that God *has* no essence (but must nonetheless

[9] *Ibid.,* 134.

be thought of as having essence, "so as not to leave the mind without any object") is possible only because it contains an ambiguity. This ambiguity permits Gilson, once he has said that "God has no essence," to ignore this proposition and to proceed to describe the essence that God truly and really has *in himself,* and not merely the meaning that God has *for us*. For the proposition "we must also keep the notion of essence" means, in effect, not only that although God *really* has no essence we must conceive his being *as if* it were an essence. Since Gilson assumes (a) the Thomistic theory of knowledge as the intentional acquisition of objects, and (b) the Thomistic theory that our rational knowledge of God attains by analogy to a real object, it follows that the essence which God is conceived as having "so as not to leave the mind without any object," is in fact also an essence which objectively and really belongs to God. Thus "we must also keep the notion of essence present to mind so as not to leave the mind without any object" means *two* different things: (a) that we must, only on account of the nature of the human mind, conceive God *as if* he had an essence, and (b) that, since God is an object of knowledge, whatever we truthfully conceive of him is truly predicable of him as *his own* objective reality. These two are, of course, mutually exclusive. They could not be integrated in a concept of God. When Gilson says that God has no essence and is beyond essence, what is at work is the idea that we conceive God *as if* he had an essence, *only* on account of the nature of the human intellect. But when he proceeds to *define* God as Subsisting Being Itself, as pure existence, as simple, as immaterial, as a person, as having all the perfections of actual being in an infinite degree—in short, as the Supreme Being who is describable as an object of thought—what is effective is the idea that the "pure existence" of God is *truthfully* conceived by us as having an essence.

There is some evidence for the view that the root of this equivocation should be traced to Gilson's attempt to reduce his own contemporary insight (namely, that essence is "proper to the being of creatures" and, hence, that God has no essence) to the doctrine of St. Thomas. To do so he had to suppose that for St. Thomas too God had no essence. Therefore, it was necessary for him to identify his own position, that "God has no essence" and is "beyond essence," with the doctrine of St. Thomas that in God there is no real distinction between essence and existence.

Yet, St. Thomas's own doctrine does not appear to be exactly that. His own words are that "God is not only his own essence . . . but also his own existence"; that "it is impossible that in God his existence should differ from his essence"; and that "God is his own existence, and not merely his own essence."[10] Taken at face value these expressions can only mean that for St. Thomas God truly has an essence, but that this essence is pure and simple *esse*. The doctrine means that God has *no specific* or *generic* essence, nor therefore a restricted *esse*. It means that for St. Thomas God has *no other* essence than to be, *esse*. But it cannot mean that God has *no* essence. In this respect Maritain appears to me as a much more reliable guide than Gilson to what St. Thomas himself seems to have thought.[11] To say that St. Thomas expressed himself as he did, instead of saying that essence is "proper to the being of creatures," or that "God has no essence," or is "beyond essence," because he wished to avoid "this uncompromising language,"[12] has the earmarks of a rationalization. The more likely reason is that to St. Thomas in the thirteenth century, as it does to Maritain today, the doctrine that God has no essence would have appeared absurd.

[10] *ST*, I, 3, 4, *et passim*.

[11] "Sur la doctrine de l'aseité divine," *Mediaeval Studies*, V (1943), 39–50.

[12] Gilson, p. 133.

On the other hand, if Gilson was not prepared to give up the hellenic metaphysical outlook beginning with the postulate of Parmenides, it may be just as well that he attempted to reduce his own insight to that of St. Thomas. For had he not stopped at St. Thomas he would have had to go all the way to Hegel. It is possible, however, that in due course neither Christian philosophy, nor Christian belief, nor the common Christian experience of God, will be formed by the conscious or unconscious assumption of Greek metaphysics. Christians should then find it logical to reason that if essence is proper to the being of creatures, then God has no essence, and therefore is not a being. And if God is not a being then he is not an object of thought and has no definition, essence, or meaning as a "thing-in-itself." In short, if God does not come into being then he is not a being, and if he is not a being then he does not exist.

This would take nothing away from the reality of God, or from either the reasonableness or the truth of the Christian faith. It would, however, take away the problem of the existence of God. Indeed, the immediate meaning of the proposition is that the existence of God is not philosophically problematical—not any more than is the existence of "extramental" being. This does not mean that the existence, or even the reality, of God is self-evident. The existence of *things* is self-evident. But unlike the reality of being, God's is a transcendent reality. He is not merely present to us; he is both present and absent. It is in this sense that the reality of God is mysterious. The problem for Christian philosophy is to explore that reality and, in the first place, to try to understand the meaning of God's simultaneous presence and absence. But this does not mean: we must determine whether an actually existing thing-in-itself corresponds to the object of thought, God. What needs to be "proven" is not that a God-being objectively exists.[13] What requires "a demonstration," for it is not immediately obvious, is God's *presence:* whether, in what sense, in what way, and with what consequences, God is *present.* Present, in the first place to himself (though this is largely a theological problem). Present, in any event, to being, present to world, present to man, present to man's faith, present to the Church, present to history, and present to the future that we create. The preoccupation with God's existence which characterized post-patristic thought, and thence post-medieval philosophy, is a result of conceiving God as an actual object of thought that is a possible objective being or thing-in-itself. But we should not place any *a priori* limits on the level of religious consciousness to which man may easily rise. In the future we may well learn to conceive God in a nobler way.

THE PERSONALITY OF GOD

Christian theism might in the future not conceive God as a person—or indeed as a Trinity of persons. I have already alluded to the reason why, namely, the conception of personality with intrinsic reference to the human mode of experience and existence: "personality is not to be conceived of apart from the act by which it creates itself."[14] Self is that which is conscious, that which can signify itself to its-self. But if a self is going to make itself into a self, if it is going to subjectify itself, it must objectify. It must objectify indeed both the world and itself. Thus,

[13] The existence (properly so called) of God would remain *morally* problematic. That is, the question would always remain open whether our self-creation will or will not proceed so as to make God to-exist-for-us.

[14] Marcel, *Homo Viator,* p. 25.

to be a subject is to be an object for oneself. Conversely, the possibility of becoming an object for oneself is what defines subjectivity, and consciousness is the process by which subjectivity comes (through objectification) into being. Now, we could hardly suppose that the ultimate reality becomes conscious and objectifies the world. This would be a regression to Hegel's evolutionary pantheism. And the substance of Hegel's doctrine, for all it owes to Scholasticism, is no more compatible with the Christian tradition than with the philosophical advances that have taken place after him.

The concept of person remains, of course, metaphorically adequate for theism. Personality has been accorded to God as long as the concept has taken its place in a philosophy for which it was "what is most perfect in all nature."[15] In our contemporary understanding of personality, however, this is no longer true. Though it remains in a sense the principal perfection of being and existence, personality is no longer aptly predicated of God partly because, as we realize the utter transcendence of the immanent Christian God, we no longer find it fitting or truly fair to the nature of God to preoccupy ourselves with granting to God *per viam remotionis et supereminentiae* the infinite degree of the creaturely perfections. Moreover, personality is no longer apt to signify any perfection transcending man, because we no longer understand personality in relation to Nature, since we do not understand being as a hierarchy of perfection and reality. It would make less sense to say that God is a super-personal being than to say that animals are infra-personal beings—for man has a historical-genetic relation to animals that he does not have to God. (I assume here, of course, that man has evolved

[15] *ST*, I, 29, 3.

from the animal, but that being, though created, has not evolved from God.) It would be, rather, like saying that nothingness is an infra-person. The statement is no doubt logically true; but it is scarcely significant.

Behind this is the fact that the very approach of the contemporary mind to an understanding of every reality, including personality, is at variance with the hellenic. The ultimate reason why God was fittingly conceived as a supra-rational person is the same as the reason why he was fittingly conceived as the super-being: that for the hellenic mind to understand any given kind of being was to find its proper place in a hierarchical scheme of being which ran from the highest to the lowest. Today we do not understand man as a rational animal—because we do not understand him as an animal to begin with. And we do not understand animals as sentient living beings for the same reason that we do not understand living beings in relation to the elementary substances totally immersed in the potency of prime matter. A person, thus, is not what is at the top of nature's organizational chart, it is just what is most immediately and directly understood. (This is why contemporary humanism asserts human values as a matter of *fact* and does not *super*-impose them upon human existence as an additional requirement over and above the requirement to be.)

Moreover, personality is the proper perfection of being, consciousness and experience at their *present* historical stage of evolution. Now, the contemporary mind does not conceive man as a body (organized and potentially having life) to which consciousness is somehow united. Consciousness is the constituent of man; it is equivalent to life and existence. It is intrinsically valuable, thus, in the same way as life and existence are valuable, that is, as an empirically verifiable matter of fact. It is, of course, what is most valuable to man: if experiential existence goes, then, as it were, all goes. And it is the highest human value in a yet deeper sense: personal conscious existence is all that we have (of ourselves) in order to *create ourselves* in time. This means that personality is the summit of man's actuality, but hardly the summit he hopes to achieve. That is evidently yet to come. For man's selfhood is what makes him transcendent. Man is the being who is sufficiently perfect to tend to transcend personality. A person is a being who knows enough to want to go beyond himself. At this point one should be referred to Teilhard de Chardin's speculations in *The Future of Man*. But the idea is scarcely new: in the most ancient Christian tradition, too, man's ultimate achievement is not found in the circumscription of his personality. It is found on the contrary in its communication and expansion beyond itself into another self, indeed, into a community of selves. The ultimate hope of the Christian faith is not that man should achieve *within himself* the act of beholding God, a vision close enough to constitute an intimate union with God; it is to achieve an intimate union with every person through a union with God *in God himself;* rather, to achieve a going-out-of-one-self-into-God, an out-going that is real enough to constitute a *self*-transformation. It is an *ek-stasis* and a *theosis,* a participation in the inner self-communication of God, that is, in his "Trinity." Personality, thus, is what we start from, not what we aspire to, namely, God.

But if God is, though not himself a person, what persons (and only persons) aspire to, it follows that man's relations to God are essentially personal. Likewise, God's relations with man are personal, for *we* are persons. To say that God is not personal, but that to which persons aspire does not reduce God to a sort of pervasive impersonal force, like gravitation. If we believe in

God we believe in the benevolence and friendship shown to persons *as such* by the openness of existence. We believe, for instance, that our own existence is a personal boon and an undeserved personal gift. Yet, the personalism of the divine-human relations might be better understood if we did not conceive the mechanics of those relations as proceeding on God's side (as they do on our own) from one—least of all from three—centers of objectification (which is the only thing that we can meaningfully and empirically call a self).

The typical experience of the disaffiliated religious person today is that "God could not possibly be a person. He must be some kind of cosmic force." This is surely a naïve view to the degree that it implies that God is less than man. But this is not all that this common expression connotes. It also means that God is, rather than a centre of being to which we are drawn, an expansive force which impels persons to go out from and beyond themselves. This expression represents an effort, born of understandable impatience, to transcend the primitive God-being, God-object and God-person of absolute theism. The truth that that crude expression so mistakenly conceives may yet be redeemed in the future by Christian theism.

THE OMNIPOTENCE OF GOD

Christian theism may in the future deal with the so-called divine attributes in much the same way as with God's being, existence, essence and personality. It is not enough to stress, as with Scholasticism, that God does not really *have* attributes (because he *is* his attributes), if we immediately proceed to conceive God as having (or, for that matter, as being) omnipotence, eternity, immateriality, infinity, immutability, omniscience, etc. In the last analysis what matters is the attributes themselves. I cannot within the limited scope of this essay speculate on how each of these attributes might be reconceptualized by Christian theism. I will consider briefly only the two which we commonly tend to think of as principal and typical, namely, omnipotence and eternity.

The question we might ask ourselves concerning God's omnipotence is not this: What are the possibilities open to a being, God, (who, having the plenitude of being, lacks by definition all limitations), for acting *upon* other beings, that is, nature? The question is rather: what can (and what, if anything, cannot) happen, once God and man enter into personal relations. The problem is not how to explain a metaphysical property of God which would have implications for us, but how to understand the reciprocal relations between man and God and, in particular, how mutual power enters into the relationship. The problem has to do, as it were, with the politics of man and God.

But once we put it this way it is difficult to retain the concept of omnipotence. Power, insofar as it means, I do not say the actuality, but even the possibility, of violence to the spontaneity of existence, does not seem to be significant to Christian belief in God. Of course, if God were a being, then *ipso facto* he would have the power to act *upon* another, and if he had the plenitude of being he would have the plenitude of power: he could act upon every being in order to determine it in any possible way consistent with the nature of God himself. But if God is not a being, then his relations to being cannot be understood in the terms of action and passion. Nevertheless, if God is a true reality truly present to being, there are true relations between God and creatures: but the politics of this relation should be understood accordingly, that is, in terms of reciprocal being-with, rather than in those of acting and being acted *upon*. The power which all reality possesses, both God's reality and our own, is real enough; for example, we do have the real power to contest the "will" of God. But power is not the basis of the personal relations between man and God, or even those of God and Nature as a whole. An omnipotent God would differ from Zeus only in that his bolts had an infinite voltage or, more exactly, in that the mechanism through which he exercised his power was not an electric fluid but, rather, the direct influence of his will upon nature.

Our frequent insistence on thinking of God as an all-powerful being is not unlike that of the child who insists on thinking of his father as the most muscular and threatening father in the neighborhood.[16] The Scholastic metaphysician may have better reasons for the same insistence, if he conceives God as pure actuality and as Supreme Being. Nevertheless, the question whether God can make a blind man to see, the dead to rise again, and a virgin to conceive—these are St. Thomas's own examples[17] —are not less misleading when answered yes than when answered no. For unless God is the Supreme Being the question is wrongheaded to begin with. The enquiry has been led astray by the concept of God which prompted it, a concept which may be explicated by such an enquiry, but not empirically reflected upon or explored.

What the Christian concept of God may perhaps stress in the future is not that, with the exception of self-contradictions, things

[16] Spinoza's warnings against creating God in our image and likeness, and his analysis of some techniques we employ to do so, (*Ethic,* Part I, Appendix), may be profitably studied apart from his own post-Scholastic, pre-Hegelian conception of God.

[17] *De Potentia,* 1, 3.

are possible to God which are impossible to nature.[18] It may instead foster the idea that, as the common phrase puts it, "wonders will never cease." And this, for two reasons. The first is that nature—and therefore what is naturally possible—should no longer be understood as it was by the Greek and the mediaeval mind. If a Christian looks at the world and understands nature through hellenic eyes, he will find it necessary to assert the omnipotence of God *over* and *against* nature. For in this view of nature, either God is necessitated by it, or it is subject to God. But in the contemporary experience nature is no longer understood as the principle which necessitates from within the operations of beings, and therefore makes them resist violence from without. We do not see nature as the source of independence and self-sufficiency which it was for Aristotle. Therefore, God does not have power *over* nature. The reason is that nature does not as such resist him.

The same idea might be put paradoxically: the God who is not being but who is present to being is much more powerful than if he were merely the omnipotent being. For instead of holding back a power reserve with which he could, whenever necessary, bend nature's refractory will, God communicates his power to nature, and so creates a nature that is of itself compliant with his will. But even this formula is grossly inadequate. It speaks of God's *will* and nature's *compliance,* which connote opposed finalities. Let us rather say that nature does not have its own natural finalities independently of God's. For being as such is not constituted by self-necessity, finality, or the independence of self-containment. It is essentially contingent. I mean, the contingency of nature is not merely that of its existence, but also that of its essence. And this essential and existential contingency

[18] *Ibid.*

of that-which-is is more vividly experienced today, even by the common man, than in any previous age. Nature is no longer the essentially un-miraculous, the intrinsically translucent to mind, the crystal-clear inflexible inner *nomos* of things which rules natural beings with the same blind fury with which *nemesis* rules human affairs. It is true, therefore, that "no word shall be impossible with God."[19] What may not be true is that the impossible is that which nature forbids.

The second reason why the idea of God's omnipotence may be transcended in the future is that the Christian conception of God might stress a point the moral and practical implications of which have been somewhat neglected: that the reality of God, implying the real possibility of a world totally open to God,[20] implies therefore a world totally open to *future creation by man*. The case is not that God can do the impossible (that is, that God has power to do that which nature cannot do), but that for God all things are possible—and that therefore with God all things are possible to man. In God nature can do *anything*. Instead of God's omnipotence, the power to overrule nature, it might be more adequate to think of the radical openness of history—an openness which not even man's freedom can annihilate—as manifesting the true extent of the "word" that is possible with God. The moral implication of this is that once it no longer has "God's omnipotence" to fall back on, our Christian conscience may be awakened to feel its adult responsibilities for taking the full initiative in "restoring all things in Christ" and for exercising its creative ingenuity in order to determine how this should be

[19] Lk. 1, 37.

[20] I take it that despite its Scholastic terminology this is the meaning of Karl Rahner's doctrine of nature as an "obediential potency" for grace, *Nature and Grace,* (London, 1963), pp. 40 ff.; cf. *Theological Investigations,* I, pp. 297–317.

done. For we will then no longer expect miracles to happen (least of all the miracle of the glorious return of the Christ upon a cloud), and we will instead believe that, unless we make it be, the Kingdom of God shall never come.[21]

THE ETERNITY OF GOD

The eternity of God should undergo a like process of de-hellenization. Existence is not measured by duration, nor is time the measure of motion. If we accept this—as we must if we accept the view that the critical analysis of temporal simultaneity in the light of scientific observations exposes it as an *a priori* concept—eternity cannot be the duration of God. For the concept of eternity as a total simultaneity is relative to the concept of time according to which the simultaneity of the parts of space is physically possible. Eternity ultimately means self-identity. The Supreme Being of Greek metaphysics requires it with absolute necessity. But if the God of the Christian faith is not conceptualized under hellenic cultural forms, eternity is, far from a necessary divine attribute, a highly unbecoming one. For an eternal God whose proper abode is a Heaven beyond creation remains essentially the Greek *theos* even if he is allowed occasional forays into time. In the Christian experience, however, God does not dip his finger into history; he totally immerses himself in it. When he visits the world he does not come slumming. He comes to stay. He arrives most concretely and decisively of all in the person of the Word in order to make earth and history his home, his permanent residence, his ever-lasting abode.

[21] This formula is equivocal. It is not intended here in the allegorical sense given to it by Marxist eschatology, but in the literal one given to it by Teilhard's.

Does this mean that God is measured by time, that he exists *in* time? Well, since time is in no way a reality *anterior* to being (that is, neither temporally anterior to being, nor in the sense that it measures the duration of being, nor that being exists in relation to it), then God does not exist in time—not any more than *man* does. Nevertheless, God is *temporal* in the same way that man is, namely, in the sense that he *makes* time. On the other hand, since God is not a being, his temporality does not create him. Unlike man, as he makes time God does not make himself; what he makes is being. Therefore, God's temporality does not consist in a self-projection out of the past towards the open possibilities of the future; let us say, then, that it consists in his being present *to* time. More precisely, since God is wholly present to all of man's and nature's time, we should say that his temporality consists in being *present to history*. The fundamental relation between man and God is found in the reality of history. It consists in the mutual presence of God and man in the *conscious* creation of the world.

Now, as I have suggested above, God's presence to nature renders nature capable of anything. If God is not the Supreme Being of the Greeks, his "omnipotence" might be better understood in terms of the absolute contingency of being, that is, the radical openness of nature and history to be fashioned into *absolutely* anything, since being is both existentially and essentially unnecessitated by anything within itself. (I stress *absolutely* in order to indicate that the creation of nature and history is not the actualization of a potency, but a genuine evolution and transformation, in which the novel and the unforeseeable can emerge, and in which the actual cannot be reduced to the potential.) Therefore, *all* history is possible. The shape of the world to come has not been determined beforehand, either by Fate, by God or by the nature of things, not even to the extent that a final causality acting on creatures by some sort of "pre-motion" inclines them towards a pre-determined, "appointed" goal. There is no divine manipulation of the puppet-strings of history, whether surreptitious or otherwise, whether co-operative or absolute. There is no pre-destination, no divinely imposed natural *ananke,* no divine command to history to unfold *kata phusis,* no *moirai;* there is not even so much as a divine policy statement prescribing the general principles by which history will happen. In a word, there is no "divine plan." For God's "omnipotence" not only means that all history is possible, it also means that all history is *free.*

All history is free and possible, in the first place, against God, given man's real freedom. His real self-creative possibilities and his true ability to create in due time any possible world mean he can actually create a history without, or against, God. The creation of such a history is what Christianity calls *sin,* and its outcome *hell,* (and evidently it is we, not God, who create it and establish its gates at the very center of the earth). This means that history can actually fail. A *real* and *eternal* (more precisely, definite, irreversible) hell is a real possibility, even if it is not a punishment willed by the Greek *dike* of God. For there is no divine decree that assures the inevitability (any more than there is one to forbid the actuality) of unending progress or the ultimate success of man. Even the definitive and utter failure of history as a whole is a real possibility, which is due to man's real role in it—though the unwavering Christian *hope* is that this real possibility will not in fact, with God's help, come to pass.

Thus, the achievement of history, the "victory" of God, is equally possible. Not only the achievement of any immediate "ideal," but even the ultimate and total achievement of history is possible—that achievement which in the Judaeo-Christian tradition is metaphorically known as the Kingdom of God, because it crowns the personal involvement of God in history. God, therefore, exists in history. To think of him as existing in a simultaneous duration above time is to force the Christian faith into a hellenic mold which is not large enough to contain it. The Christian God's substance is not above history; is the substance of history itself.

I do not mean, of course, Hegel's History. M. Garaudy has rightly said that such a history cannot be called God.[22] Nor, on the other hand, *pace* Garaudy, should such a history be called *man,* since history is no more the self-actualization of an original potentiality called *matter* than the self-actualization of an original potentiality called *Absolute Spirit* or *logical necessity.* There is no antinomy between the concept of God as history and the historical creativity of man. All that this means is that history is free—free with a freedom that is not reducible to man's free creation of history. For man indeed makes history, but history is not reducible to what man freely makes of it. History is made by man, but in the presence of God. Conversely, God is personally present to man in history. *With* God indeed all things, all history, is possible to man.

It may not be inappropriate to add that Marxists are only consistent with their atheism when, interpreting the truth of Engel's thesis that "men themselves make their history, only they do so in a given environment which conditions it, and on the basis of actual relations already existing,"[23] they take this proposition to mean that, in the last analysis, history is not really made by man's true total and creative freedom, but by a Stoic

[22] *From Anathema to Dialogue,* p. 95.
[23] Friedrich Engels, *Letter to Starkenburg,* January 25, 1894.

"freedom" consisting in man's wise resignation, his spontaneous willingness to conform himself to what must in any event be.[24] This may only show once again that Marxism is in the line which harks back through Hegel, Spinoza and Descartes to hellenized Christianity. More to the point, the paradoxical result of failing to see that the freedom of history cannot be exhaustively accounted for by human freedom, is to reduce human freedom to the necessity of a History which has no reality other than that of predestinating man. Conversely, man's total freedom to create history can be guaranteed only by the admission of God's historical presence to human history. Or, if I may put the matter polemically: Engels' thesis can be literally and fully maintained only within Christian theism, and its ultimate inconsistency with atheism can be evaded only by emasculating its force and by making it mean that it is really history that makes men. But it should not be put polemically. Christianity has its own problems to look after. Let me then simply advance the suggestion that Christian theism may in the future conceive God as a historical presence, indeed as History, yet a history that would destroy neither human freedom nor God's reality precisely because such a God would not be eternal.

There is no need to elevate History to the level of supratemporal reality (Marxism), or to humble temporal reality to the status of an infra-divine succession of spatial events (Scholasticism). The events that happen, once God makes himself present to human history, are contingent—both on man's and on God's side. The full force of this is best appreciated from the fact that the historical events which mark the very origin of Christianity,

[24] Friedrich Engels, *Anti-Dühring,* (London, 1940 edn.), p. 128. Cf. G. V. Plekhanov, *The Individual's Role in History,* (New York, 1940), pp. 15–18.

the conception and birth of Jesus, his subsequent life and his ultimate death on the cross, are held by the Christian faith to have been contingent events. The "saving events" were events none of which *had* to happen, events all of which had to be *willed* before they could happen at all.[25] God the Word, in the person of Jesus, did not have to take the unattractive form of a human embryo, and give morning sickness to his mother, and go through with the joyful but messy business of being born. He did not have to become involved in sectarian religious disputes, or in a fist fight, or make himself so thoroughly obnoxious that in the end he got himself killed. None of these things had to happen, none of them had been fated or decreed in advance. But these things did happen, and the contingency with which they did happen is significant. For all these were perfectly ordinary, everyday temporal, indeed in a sense trivial, events. Well, *that* is the kind of event in which revelation, incarnation, redemption and salvation did in fact take place. *That* is the mode of God's historical presence to man.

It is indeed because concrete historical events, even as involving God, are in fact contingent, and because any involvement whatever of God with man is universally and in principle contingent, that atheism must always remain possible as a logical and consistent attitude towards reality. What Christians may realize better in the future is that, as man's consciousness develops, we must conceive God as historical *or not at all.* We must understand God either as present in history, or otherwise as altogether absent to

[25] The basis of the Catholic cult of Mary is that the *first* of all these events had to be willed by her, a human being, before the others could be willed at all. Therefore, Marian *hyperdulia* is certainly due and proper. It seems to me that the difficulty with the usual Marian devotions is not that they *exaggerate* Mary's historical importance to the Christian faith, but that they *distort* it.

man. That may be why to the same degree that we have in the past discouraged the world's (and our own) understanding of God as present in history, we have facilitated the dis-belief in God of modern times (as well as our own non-theoretical atheism).

THE BASIS OF MAN'S RELIGIOUS RELATIONS WITH GOD

Underlying all that has been said above has been the assumption that for Christian theism God is not a reality of primarily metaphysical significance. He is rather a reality of primarily ontic import. It is not God as a "separate substance" but as self-communicating and thus as present to man, that matters—it being understood, however, that the God who is present to man is God himself, in the fullness of his nature, for the Word of God that comes to us is *homoousios, consubstantialis Patri*. The hellenic cultural form of Christianity, however, has made it difficult for us to realize the difference between man's relations with the God of metaphysics and his relations with the God of the Christian religion. Conceiving the Christian God as the First and Supreme Being of Greek metaphysics (with additional properties and activities inaccessible to reason "yet necessary for salvation" having been, moreover, revealed), we have consequently conceived the fundamental religious relation between God and man to be one of *ascendance-submission*. But as Christian theism is dehellenized the Christian faith may recast the meaning of religion in terms that do not *at all* imply God's ascendancy over man, or man's submission to God.

The reasons why ascendance-submission has been paramount in religion are too complex to permit analysis here. I will but mention, for instance, that there is a certain warrant in the Gospels, like Jesus' address to God as *abba,* for conceiving God's relation to man as paternalistic. This in turn was conditioned by cultural factors such as the Hebrew culture of Jesus' own mind and thought. The traditional concept of God of the Old Testament deserves particular mention especially insofar as this concept had primitive roots or acquired later hellenic accretions which might have initiated the shift from a strictly metaphorical fatherhood-filiation, signifying ontic relations between man and God, to a metaphysical principality-subjection, signifying metaphysical ones. But the perpetuation and theoretical justification of the idea that the metaphorical fatherhood of God is superimposed upon a properly analogical relation of metaphysical superiority-inferiority—this had to wait until God's proper name became one of a metaphysical nature, namely Being, He Who is.[26] This idea, already present in the early Fathers, found its culmination in Scholasticism with the doctrine that "this name, He Who is, is the most proper" name of God.[27] With the adoption of Greek philosophy came the split of the *ontic* relations of God and man into the *metaphysical,* which are antecedent, and the *moral,* which are consequent. Henceforth the hierarchy of being was the principal and *antecedent* determinant of the relations between man and God. Adoration, for example, was due to God in strict justice: most basically of all man owed worship to God because God was the Supreme Being. To this basic fact of man's religious life was *appended* a revealed, Chris-

[26] The hellenic influence on the Old Testament to which I have alluded above pertains only to certain later books. I am assuming here the most common contemporary exegesis of Exod. 3, 14, and related texts, which make Gilson's understanding of it, following St. Thomas, exceedingly suspect.

[27] *ST,* I, 13, 11.

tian *modifier,* namely, those aspects of God taught by Scripture which determine, (by way of terminal perfection,) as it were the *moral* relations of charity-gratitude, mercy-piety, forgiveness-repentance, etc.

The tendency thus built into Christian belief (and later transmitted to its early modern secularized theologies) to sunder faith and morals, theory and practice, contemplation and action, is a self-contradiction of historical Christianity, and when Marx opposed it[28] he was perhaps unwittingly voicing the Christian experience of God. By the same token, M. Garaudy is substantially justified when he isolates a single sentence from *Quadragesimo anno*—it might have been *Rerum novarum*—and discards the rest (which, at bottom, merely tempered it) in order to symbolize that historically Christianity has tended to subordinate morality to man's metaphysical Fate—albeit a Fate which allows itself to be swayed by supplication and sacrifice:

> Since Constantine, the teaching of the Church, in its official form and during the major part of its history, has curbed or combated the struggles of the oppressed by locating in another world the conquest of justice, freedom and happiness, by bestowing a legitimacy as of divine right on the established order, and by teaching resignation in the face of exploitation and oppression. . . . [The] masters of Christian thought have made all class domination legitimate: slavery, serfdom, the salary system. . . . [In modern times] the basic thesis [of this doctrine] will be developed in all its generality by Pope Pius X on December 18, 1903: "Human society as established by God is made up of unequal elements. . . . Accordingly, it is in conformity with the order of human society as established by God that there be rulers and ruled, employers and employees, rich and poor, learned and ignorant, nobles and plebeians."
>
> There evidently flows from this thesis a social doctrine based on

[28] Most of familiarly perhaps in the eleventh of the *Theses on Feuerbach,* "The philosophers have only *interpreted* the world . . . ; the point, however, is to *change* it," which calls to mind the exhortation to Christians to be "doers of the word," Jas. 1, 22.

resignation. The encyclical *Quadragesimo anno* (1931) explicitly drew this conclusion: "The workers will accept without rancor the place which Divine Providence has assigned to them".[29]

But here, again, it would be easy to be anachronistic. The subordination of morality to Fate—or to Providence (*pronoia*),[30] the technical concept devised by the Stoics as the final philosophical form of the mythological *moirai*—was no corruption of Christianity. Indeed, if we go sufficiently far back it was at one time not even a gross inadequacy of it. It was normal as long as the state of human consciousness made it normal to base all interpersonal relations on the superiority-inferiority of essences. If this was true of father and son, husband and wife, elder and younger, ruler and citizen, noble and plebeian, master and servant, then why not God and man? Thus M. Garaudy's remarks are in general as valid as Marx's earlier ones—or as valid as those previously made to the same point in the sixteenth century by the Spanish Dominican Bartolomé de las Casas. But the expectation that St. Paul might have reasonably entertained the abolition of slavery would be, I believe, not inspired by a sound sense of history.

On the other hand, man and the world have long ago changed. The perpetuation of the concept of God which permitted such things has been, since no later than the eighteenth century, inadequate, to say the least. How long we today, in the nuclear age, can persist in this inadequacy without crossing the line into corruption and infidelity can be left for each Christian conscience to decide for itself. Since I have the firm hope that this line will not be crossed, I think that the Christian theism of the future might so conceive God as to find it possible to look back with amusement on the day when it was thought particularly ap-

[29] *Op. cit.,* pp. 97–98.
[30] On the equivalence of Providence and Fate, see *ST,* 116, 1.

propriate that the believer should bend his knee in order to worship God. For when the eyes of the Christian faith remove their hellenic lenses, what continues to appear sacred about hierarchical relations as such? What remains, of any transcendental importance, about the mere facts of relative superiority-inferiority, wherever they may be found? Is not the point that superiority-inferiority, however real, is no longer an adequate basis for interpersonal relations? And would it not even seem somewhat unbecoming for the God of the Christian tradition to take pleasure in the kind of interpersonal relation that even we human beings are beginning to find unworthy of ourselves?

The Church's "crisis of authority," feared by not a few, may be at bottom the crisis of absolute theism; and they (mostly stigmatized as "conservatives") are possibly right who think that the Church's decision to recognize the reality of freedom and conscience can only result in the eventual disappearance of Christianity in the form in which we have known it since primitive times. They are quite possibly right who estimate that resistance to, or impatience with, ecclesiastical authoritarianism betrays resistance to, or impatience with, God's own authority as traditionally understood. The trouble is that it is becoming increasingly difficult for many Christians—and their numbers proliferate daily—to believe in the authoritarian God as traditionally understood. Indeed, some find themselves compelled by their Christian faith, and constrained by their loyalty to Christ, to his Church, and to the living History in which they live and breathe, positively and actively to *dis-believe* in a divine being who is only in degree and in detail different from primitive deities or from philosophical gods. They find themselves compelled by their Christian faith to *dis-believe* in a Supreme

Being, in a God behind whose kindness and generosity to man stands a supreme, omnipotent and eternal will.

If the religious experience that requires a less primitive concept of God is genuinely in the line of the true Christian faith—and time will surely tell whether it is—then it is possible that Christianity will in the future judge that the conception of God as the *acme* of metaphysical supremacy and religious ascendancy fails to do him justice and to lead to the most adequate form and level of worship of which man is already capable. We may yet judge that we have not sufficiently well appreciated in the past that to place God at the summit of creation is to place him in an insufficiently noble station in the world. To say that God is the highest and the first being, and that he has to the infinite degree all the creaturely perfections, may not be nearly enough to begin to approximate the transcendent reality of God. To multiply infinities is not the way to transcend them.

To conceive God in terms other than superiority-inferiority, and his relations with us in terms other than ascendance-submission, does not, however, take away from any of our ultimate obligations. It takes away, least of all, the need for humility. It does not diminish the moral obligation to blush, avert our eyes, and feel sick to our stomachs as we watch the spectacle that severally and collectively we make of ourselves. But humility is not the recognition of our inferiority to God's superiority. It is, as St. Theresa of Ávila, with her usual good sense once said, the recognition of the truth. And the truth is that the God of Christian belief is not the apex of the pyramid of creation or of the hierarchy of being, not only because he is *beyond* creation and being but also because he is *within* creation and being. He seems rather to rule himself by the principle of noblesse oblige, so that being the noblest he is also the humblest reality,[31] not having hesitated to give man the freedom that renders him capable of true personal friendship and partnership in the creation of history and world.

In sum, God's grace and charity are not superadditions to his metaphysical nature. God is not charitable; he *is* charity, *Deus caritas est.*[32] By the same token, worship might not be understood as the just rendering of homage. (It may be significant that religion is the last area within the Christian world where the institution of homage is consciously and unashamedly retained.) Worship might be better understood as the rendering of ourselves present to the presence of God, whether in the interior prayer which sends no message to God but which receives his presence, or in the public and common ceremonies which visibly, audibly and sensibly unite us through our collective presence to each other in the presence of the present God.

THE SUPERNATURAL CHARACTER OF GOD

Finally, the Christian concept of God may develop in the direction of shedding its supernatural character. But this would scarcely mean that we would conceive God as a "natural" being in the hellenic or Scholastic senses of the term. Indeed, this would not be so much a development in our concept of God as in our concept of nature.

As I have already indicated, the concept of the supernatural, though crucially effective in shaping the face of Christianity once it came into play, actually originated in certain apologetic concerns of Scholasticism. It is not of itself an intrinsic part of the

[31] Cf. *Philippians* 2, 6–8.
[32] *1* Jn. 4, 8.

Christian faith. What is absolutely fundamental to the Christian experience is that which is conceptualized in the doctrine of *grace*. This doctrine is intimately connected with several points already mentioned, and in particular with the belief that the gratuitous self-communication of God to us, once received by us lives in us and, as it were, vivifies us. God's indwelling in us constitutes a sort of "principle" of our religious and "spiritual" life. As proceeding within God himself this is the Spirit of God. But as immanent in us, the Spirit of God is known as the "gift" (*donum*) of God. (The distinction is often made between God's Gift itself and its immediate effect in us, created *grace,* a perfection of our nature; but this may be abstracted from here). The importance of this doctrine for Christian theism can hardly be exaggerated. In God's nature as *charity* or self-gift (*charis,* the Greek root of this word, means the same as a freely given [*gratis*] gift), that is, in his nature as self-communicating and self-giving superabundance is found the rationale of belief in God as a friendly and benevolent pervasive presence in every reality which constantly manifests itself to us and which should normally produce the Christian's appreciation of existence, his enjoyment of life, and the consequent moral obligation of charity towards our fellow man. We are "commanded" to love our neighbor for the love of God. The ethics of Christianity depend wholly upon the theism of charity. And our existence, our endowments, our attainments and, finally, our moral status vis-à-vis God and the relation of mutual friendship between man and God—all these have always been experienced by Christians as gratuitous gifts directly received from God or, at very least, dependent on such gratuitous gifts.

But to the degree that the hellenic understanding of nature was shared by Christians—and very especially from the twelfth century onwards—Christian theology became persuaded that natures were intelligible only insofar as they were inwardly necessitated. It became imperative to safeguard the gratuity of grace, which appeared to be imperilled by the necessity of nature as discerned by the findings of contemporary scientific enquiry. (It would be an exaggeration, but an instructive one, to say that Scholasticism was generated out of this antinomy between faith and reason.) The solution was to interpret God's gratuitous relations with man as pertaining to an order of reality "above" the natural order, which "perfected" nature without destroying or taking away from it in its own "natural" order. This doctrine thus safeguarded not only the gratuity of grace, but also the hellenic autonomy of nature. Nature remained constituted in its own order of intelligibility by its necessity, while grace perfected it by "elevating" it to a supernatural state. It cannot be doubted that this was a most fruitful theological development. But its assumptions pertain not only to the order of Christian faith. Some of the crucial ones belong strictly to the order of hellenic thought.

As long as two generations ago, Maurice Blondel had already understood well that the insistence of the "veterists" (as he would later call them with obvious allusion to the "modernists"), upon the traditional doctrine of the supernatural, despite the obsolescence of the Aristotelian-Thomistic concept of nature, was in the last analysis no more satisfactory a contemporary solution to the problem than that provided by the diametrically opposite movement, which attempted to reduce the order of grace to that of nature. The difficulty, as he rightly discerned, lay in their *common* assumptions concerning nature:

> Does the supernatural consist, as the extrinsicist thesis implies, in a notional relationship determined and imposed by God, there being

no link between natural and supernatural but only an ideal juxtaposition of heterogeneous and even impenetrable elements which only the obedience of our minds can bring together? In that case the supernatural subsists only if it remain extrinsic to the natural, and if it is proposed to us from outside, its whole value residing in the fact that it is *above* nature. Or can it be reduced, as the historicist thesis implies, to being no more than another name for the divine or for a sort of concentration of it in nature itself, so that, if it is not entirely confused with nature, that is because after all one must have a word for the phase at present reached by our religious aristocracy? In short, should it be regarded more or less as an intellectual privilege which only exists as such, in opposition to, and as external to, the common state? Or is it a love-relationship which insinuates a new order into the normal order—where man is and can only be *servus Dei*—one in which the slave can become the friend, the brother, and even *tanquam Deus Dei;* so that, through this relationship, through grace, all men are made to feel, if not the spirit of adoption lost by the first fault, at least a profound sense of unrest, a mysterious hunger of the soul? This is an order, a state, all the more freely infused into nature because it cannot be confused with nature. For the 'state of nature' is a pure abstraction which does not exist and never has existed; in studying the nature of man as it actually is, we do not get to know the 'state of nature' any more than we can abstract, in our lives, the radical and universal penetration of something which will always prevent us from finding our equilibrium in the merely human order.[33]

Evidently, what Blondel was groping for was a re-conceptualization of the "supernatural," rather, of *grace,* in the light of the contemporary understanding of the total contingency of nature.

In recent times, as philosophy has diverged more and more from its Greek presuppositions, and as nature and essence have ceased to be understood as intelligible necessities, the concept of the supernatural has lost its usefulness for Christian theism. This is one concrete reason why, as I have already suggested, since

[33] *History and Dogma,* Dru-Trethowan trans., (New York, 1964), pp. 283–284. (Italics in the original.)

the mainstream of Catholic *philosophy* has remained Scholastic and hence unsympathetic to the contemporary understanding of nature, Catholic *theology*, especially in those circles that have consciously abandoned Scholasticism (for example, the Teilhardians), or in those specialties that were never dominated by it (for example, in scriptural studies), has increasingly turned to non-Christian, secular thought for philosophical help. In any event, the result of conceiving nature as essentially, and not merely existentially, contingent can be readily appreciated. Once we so understand it, the concept of the supernatural becomes insufficient to safeguard the meaningfulness of the traditional and essential Christian belief in the contingency and gratuity of all the relations between man and God. The distinction between the natural and the supernatural becomes a mere play on words, irrelevant to reality. In the alternative view grace continues to be what Christian belief always held it was, but nature ceases in every way to be opposed to grace: it is naturally apt to receive grace,[34] because that is how it was in fact created. Since nature is essentially contingent, deriving its intelligibility from its factuality and historicity, nature is historically, not metaphysically, related to grace. Grace is thus understood as a historical fact, God's presence to man, which existentially qualifies the historical intelligibility of nature in a definitive way.

Although one might wish to avoid the terms *naturalism* and *secularism* on account of their historical association with philosophies that are not easily reconcilable with the Christian faith, the fact is that Catholic thought and experience tends with increasing rapidity to interpret Christian belief in the terms of the temporal history of natural entities. But it is most important to note that in this formula the term *natural* is the equivalent of *historically factual*. (I should incidentally remark that this has

[34] Cf. note 20, above.

profound implications for an understanding of the relation of faith and scientific enquiry, and in particular for the problems of the nature and methods of Christian philosophy and theology.) Grace transmutes mere spatio-temporal *facts* into ultimate, religious *truths;* it transposes, as it were, abstract point-events into three-dimensional, real-life happenings in their full ontic reality. The difference between a "natural" and a "supernatural" event or reality (or between the "secular" and the "religious" explanation thereof), concerning any order whatever of reality, from the amoeba to the ziggurat (or concerning any order whatever of explanation, from Archaeology to Zoology), is not in the abstract spatio-temporal *content* but in the existential historical *form* of the event or reality (or of the ascertained explanation thereof). Hence, a non-religious order of either everyday experience or scientific explanation lacks faith, professes to have the rigor of black and white and, wishing to be absolute and self-sufficient, excludes revelation. Christian experience, whether common-sense or scientific, on the other hand, is colored by faith. It imports belief into knowledge, not to judge it but to interpret it in relation to existence; not in order to argue *a priori* what is and what is not true, or even what might and might not be true, but in order to discover the inner meaning, or the fuller sense, of the one and only "natural" truth. In this sense, too, it would not be inexact—though, to repeat, somewhat equivocal and misleading—to say that Christian speculation and Christian everyday experience are becoming naturalistic and secular.

Against this background I suggest that in the future we may not feel the need to conceive God as a super-natural being. If we discard the hellenic view of nature, the Christian God no longer must, in order to remain free, gracious and freely self-giving, perform super-natural feats, undertake super-natural functions and roles, or enjoy super-natural status. The traditional

Christian faith could then be reasserted under new forms which might make more meaningful and vivid the concepts of grace and charity than the theory of the super-natural has done in the past. The problem of evil, for instance, might be more adequately solved in the future if, as we conceive God's gracious self-communication, we do not experience the philosophical need to shackle ourselves with the Stoic-Scholastic concepts of pro-vidence or foresight (*pro-noia*). We might then proceed without casting God in the ancient roles of *Clotho* the spinner of life-threads, or *Lachesis* the dispenser of lots.[35] In brief, God's grace may be understood as the self-bestowal of the ultimate reality, hence as the source of faith and inspiration, and of existence and creativity, no longer God's cornucopia of immaterial plenty, but the *alpha* and *omega* of consciousness and *praxis,* existence and life.

THE NAME OF GOD

One may well wonder whether the Christian faith, if it develops in the direction here suggested, would experience the need to retain the traditional name, *God,* to refer to the ultimate

[35] The understandable hesitation of the Scholastic doctrine which equates Providence and "the cause of Fate," (*ST,* I, 116, 2, ad 1)—ultimately reflected in the inability after several centuries to resolve the controversies on predestination—is apparent at a fundamental level in the fact that, somewhat illogically, the Christian God has never been cast in the unqualified role of the third Fate, *Atropos* the inflexible. St. Thomas avoided making Fate absolutely inflexible by supposing that the inflexibility of Fate, though real, is only hypothetically necessary. That is, Fate is not inflexible of its own nature, but only because necessity "is allotted" to it, "*fatum . . . immobilitatem sortitur,*" (*ST,* I, 116, 3), insofar as it is subject to God. Thus, Fate is not inflexible of itself, but only insofar as it is itself fated by God. The antinomy of this doctrine helps explain much of the subsequent history of Christian doctrine and practice, including certain inadequacies of the social and other moral doctrines of the Church in modern times.

presence and reality in which it believes. Why, indeed, retain the traditional designation, if it no longer means the same thing?

I could not say anything on the subject that had not been better said already by Harvey Cox.[36] But because some Catholics might be sensitive on the point I should like to recall St. Thomas's observation that "wise people do not worry about names."[37] Precisely as name, God's name matters little. It is not truly a Holy Name, and we may please ourselves whether we retain it or not. It is our own invention, not God's, and what we have invented we may improve upon. All that matters for the development of the Christian faith is whether we stand ready to discard whatever might come between man and God. For we should not believe in God's name, any more than we should believe in faith: we should believe only in God.

In the light of the conception of God sketched above it might well be thought somewhat unfitting to call God by a proper name (and there can be little doubt that *God* has become a proper name). Moreover, though names often stick for chance reasons, names that should be dear to us should be kept alive only because they are meaningful—and, speaking of contemporary man in general, the name *God* is possibly not a particularly meaningful one. On the other hand, name-calling, as distinct from name-predicating, is more often guided by vagaries than by design. There would be little point in putting forward a new name for God—even if anyone had particularly sagacious proposals to suggest. The likelihood is that Christians will do what comes naturally to them. We have an excellent—if negative—instance of this in the case of an ancient and traditional Christian name for God which has great historical importance,

[36] *The Secular City,* (New York, 1965), pp. 265–268.
[37] *II Sent.,* 3, 1, 1.

but which has lost its meaningfulness so completely we no longer recognize it as a name. I refer to the name *Light*. It made a great deal of sense in the fourth century—especially to the hellenic mind—but it hardly makes any today. It has therefore become an empty sound, despite the fact that by the Church's command it is repeated by every Catholic at least once a week.

A more likely possibility than devising new names for God might be that of devising new ways to speak about God without naming him at all. Given the transcendence of the immanent Christian God and the inevidence of the Christian experience of him, any name whatever tends to lose usefulness and meaningfulness by sheer repetition and the mere passage of time. But given also the stage of human civilization that we have reached, it may be that Christianity is now offered the opportunity to take a new tack. In the future it may become increasingly possible for the Christian faith at all levels—everyday belief, theological and philosophical investigation, authoritative and non-authoritative teaching and preaching, and liturgy and catechesis —to reserve a special place for *silence* in *discourse* about God. We may all have to learn that to say certain things well it is sometimes better to leave others unsaid. No doubt, it is very difficult to determine where the balance lies: the point is that there *is* a balance, and that it is perfectly possible to talk too much as well as too little, even in the case of God. It may be that saying about God all we can, but being also as silent as we can regarding his name, might increase the meaningfulness of whatever religious experience we may wish to convey to others, to ourselves and to God.

In any event, greater circumspection in our use of the name God might not be unprofitable. It sometimes seems that we—I mean, the Christian Church—have come to use the name of God, if not with recklessness, at least with some abandon. Yet, names are somewhat like icons. No one could seriously propose at this late date another iconoclastic crusade, but the fact is we generally find it more congenial today to do without picture images of God than used to be our natural wont. The same might be true of word images. Our renewed observance of the second Sinaitic commandment—motivated not so much by the same considerations that inspired Old Testament man as by the desire to render God's presence more immediate to us—might well be taken as the symbol and sign of the future development of Christian theism.

Index